Recollections From an Outback Sheep Station

# Acknowledgements

I give warm heartfelt thanks to Stephen Matthews and Ginninderra Press for publishing my memoir. It was one of the most delightful shocks I have ever experienced when Stephen came back to me with a 'Yes' he wanted to go ahead with publication. I shall be forever grateful for this wonderful opportunity. I thank Christina Houen for her invaluable editorial assistance and of course Debbie Lee for seeing *Recollections From an Outback Sheep Station* through to publication.

Loraine Saunders

# Recollections From an Outback Sheep Station

*Recollections From an Outback Sheep Station*

All rights reserved. This book or any portion thereof may not be reproduced or used in any manner whatsoever without the express written permission of the publisher except for the use of brief quotations in a book review.

Paperback ISBN: 978 1 76109 699 0

Copyright © text Loraine Saunders 2024

Cover image: The cover photograph shows dorpers at Puttapa sheep station. I thank Graham Ragless for his permission to use the photograph. I am in the foreground contemplating life.

First published 2024 by
Ginninderra Press
PO Box 2 Bentleigh VIC 3204
www.ginninderrapress.com.au

# Contents

## Part One
Where the Hell Are We Going? — 9
Dirt Road to Amirda — 14
Meeting the Aussie Landed Gentry — 21
Is that Halloween Wallpaper? — 27
The Water Run — 34
Guns, Managers and Mistresses — 39
Trying to Talk to My Mother — 44
Gun Shots for Real — 47
Who's Worse, My Mother or the Creepy Campers? — 50
Please Don't Take Me to Mount Remote — 56
Irrational Worries or Legitimate Fears? — 60
What do Aussies Have Against Whole Words? — 65
A Local Speaks to Us! — 72
The Six-year Drought Was Coming to an End — 76
Our Driveway Has Turned Into the Rapids — 83
Mud, Devastation and the Clean-up Operation — 86
Will the Crows or Eagles Eat Us First? — 90
What is Covid? — 99

## Part Two
Stuck on the Station — 109
Mustering the Sheep — 117
From Calm to Chaos — 122
Musterers Who Can't Ride — 126
The Hills Are Alive with the Sound of… — 132
The Homestead Turns into Downton Abbey – Yes, M'lady — 137
Carrying on Like a Pork Chop — 140

| | |
|---|---|
| Gay Rams | 145 |
| Chuck Relationships: Is Steve Making Me Crestfallen? | 149 |
| Broken Hearts and Mending Relationships | 155 |
| Months Pass by and I'm Talking to Spiders | 157 |
| Am I Going to Comedy School? | 161 |
| Getting Ready for Clown School | 164 |
| All Booked for Adelaide | 167 |
| The Bates Motel: I Get to Meet Norman | 172 |
| I Want a Life as Full as Cid's Wallet | 175 |
| Merino Sheep Are Woolly As… | 178 |
| Up a Gum Tree | 183 |
| I Finally Make it to the Adelaide Hills | 185 |
| My First Day at Clown School | 188 |
| Not Those Two Again! | 190 |
| We Need to Have a Conversation | 192 |
| I Know There Are No Lions in the Creek, Right? | 197 |
| Only Mad Dogs and Cricketers Go Out in the Midday Sun | 199 |
| I'm Getting a Stand-up Gig on TV! | 202 |
| The Aussie Lingo | 204 |
| Can Rain Be Funny? | 206 |
| I'm No Longer a Pommie But a PoMFA | 208 |
| Oh God, Must I Do Another Muster? | 211 |
| The Hokey Cokey Yard Dance | 215 |
| Am I the Barmy Army or Just Plain Barmy? | 220 |
| Sheep Shearers Are Sooooo Cool | 224 |
| It's Aussie Cricketers Who Are Barmy | 226 |
| The Horses – and Horrible Symbolism | 228 |
| It's Time to Go, But Where? | 231 |

# Part One

## Where the Hell Are We Going?

It was New Year's Day, and we were driving north towards a never-ending line of mountains on the horizon. I thought we were still headed for the Adelaide Hills. South Australia was new to me. I didn't know the Adelaide Hills were long behind us – in fact, they were on fire, but thanks to our busted radio and our Internet signal being out of range, I didn't know that either. Nor did I know that leaving my husband was about to get a whole lot harder, not least because when you both love and hate your partner, nothing is fricken easy.

So, while we were chugging up to that distant mountain range, I was imagining how I would say 'adios amigo' to Steve while serving out the end of my wedded sentence on an Australian country estate. I was going to where the meadows were green, the sheep woolly and the shearers many and muscly (so I was hoping). Steve was going to where he could put off thinking about what to do with the rest of his going-nowhere life for another few months, and I could squeeze in one last new experience before slipping back to England to start over as a free single soul.

Steve drove the Mitsubishi Canter with a Winnebago caravan stuck on its back. I had long ceased to drive anything because he was too nervous a passenger. But in this case, I couldn't legally drive the 'medium-rigid' vehicle, which I named the Bus. The huge windows gave panoramic views of the ever-changing Aussie landscape, spectacular along those gloriously empty roads. However, the Bus was coming to the end of its life. It was due for retirement because it was a carbon-spewing emissions bandit from the 80s that would keep Greta Thunberg awake at night. At many a caravan park, we had spoiled people's breakfasts when Steve cranked up the Bus. The corroding engine blew out great clouds of soot into our neighbours' awning. They'd shake a fist and swear at us as we left them choking on fumes.

So our year-plus road trip was over. The thrills of new experiences had been dwindling for a while, at least for me. I was like a drug addict who'd taken too many hits: the highs were harder to reach. I was no longer awed by stargazing, or delighted in being the only swimmers in an empty sea. Plus, we were more and more in campsites, and those places I came to loathe, populated as they are by grey, nosy nomads. Then there's the slopping-out in the mornings, prison fashion… I was over it. I longed to take a dump without having to listen to Jane and Mary discussing Bert's new colostomy bag, or where they could get a hair appointment, and to get away from slippery, hair-clogged shower blocks, shitty dunnies and queues for…just about everything, to say nothing of new faces and conversations about the same bloody thing: 'Where you from? How long you been travelling? Where you headed for?' Mind your own damn business.

I yearned to wake up without pins and needles in my arm from being squashed against the panel of the narrow upper bed chamber in the Bus. It was like sleeping in a coffin. I had the feeling, with my nose too close to the ceiling, that I was buried alive. Before, the throbbing arm was only a mild discomfort, but it became an unbearable morning irritation. As did wanting to get up without bumping my head or having to slide over sleepy Steve like a sniper over a dead buddy. Something I found fun before, a distraction, part of the adventure. Now I wanted to wake up alone and not be told what I was going to do for the day. Sure, I would be asked, 'What do you fancy doing?' However, until I gave the activity that he had in mind, we were going nowhere. In any case, when you're doing stuff with people who are exhausting your nerves, it doesn't matter what you do – the whole day sucks.

I thought I'd outsmarted Steve when I got him a stint on a vineyard-cum-sheep station – the place I thought we were heading to. The ad was posted on a 'Country Jobs' site. I heard of it through a couple of grey nomads talking about how suitable it would be for their grandson who was looking for station experience but nothing too remote. The couple had been bugging the crap out of me for days. They were white-haired, visor-wearing, sneaker-sporting gits of about 90, way too fit for their age, who were serious space invaders. If they peeled an orange, I got the zest in my eyes. They broke camp etiquette by driving-in their Winnebago. They were supposed to back into their slot. Sounds petty, but hear me out. Owing to their driving in, their door faced ours. Strangers' doors facing each other is a camp no-no unless you're part of the same group. But they didn't care about rules. They set up their chairs and table right opposite to ours, stealing our privacy. Consequently, we'd sit every morning and night close enough to tickle each other's knees if we felt so inclined. The spiteful satisfaction I felt when I heard Steve saying that he'd got the position on the vineyard station almost made me forget my secret plans for escape.

As our journey to those distant mountains progressed, I was picturing a pretty, ivy-covered homestead overlooking rows of grape-laden vines, and thinking of all the gratis Shiraz that would complement dinner. Oh, and we'd have high-end accommodation with a spa bath and a four-poster bed – I was in heaven already. I would ring my mother and put a smile on her face: 'Here I am, safe and settled for a few months and then I'll come see you…' And won't I have a surprise for you when I announce I'm there to stay? What you said to me in Germany before you boarded your flight is finally happening. I can hear you now: Steve isn't right for you. Come home.

Yes, I was looking forward to staying in one place. I would finish that novel I'd been making so many notes for. My first psychological thriller and domestic noir – a reworking of my own marital discord – in case you were wondering. Then I would book that long-promised return flight to Heathrow, London. But first, I'd get to meet an example of the Antipodean landed gentry, another story for the family to hear about. I wondered if this well-to-do couple would be a standoffish lord and lady of the kind who owned like estates in England. Perhaps more down-to-earth. She was probably a country girl who sat on committees, baked award-winning cakes, and made pots of preserve from the fruits of her verdant gardens just like Maggie Beer – maybe it was Maggie Beer!

But I'm getting off track.

Soon, our journey towards those mountains (clearly not hills any more) was giving me concern. I was getting upset by the growing number of dead roos and emus along the roadside, although the giant wedge-tailed eagles feasting on them was something to see. I noticed we were motoring right alongside the mountains and the prevailing colour, like the eagles, was brown. All the greenery was gone, as had all the traffic. The never-ending road was strangely empty for one so close to a major city. We were starting to see a lot of sheep and cattle either side too.

I asked Steve how much longer the journey was going to take.

He said, 'There's a little bit to go yet.' He shot me a smile and raised his eyebrows.

I knew that when Steve smiles at me while raising his eyebrows, there's something he's not telling me.

'We've left the Adelaide Hills behind, haven't we?' I said, indicating the mountains.

Steve threw back his head and laughed. When he stopped laughing, he said, nodding at the mountains, 'That's the Flinders Ranges. Our new home.'

'What?' I asked, feeling my brow contract so hard that the wrinkles might split.

He said, 'You always wanted a true, what would you say, a "non-touristy" Aussie experience?' He glanced at me.

'Ye-es.'

Fixing his eyes back on the road, he said, 'You're gonna get one. We're heading into the real outback.'

I fired questions at him, like why hadn't he told me about the job-change?

But he stopped me, saying, 'Let's play I Went to the Weird Porn Shop and bought… You start.'

When I didn't answer, he said, 'Come on, I went to the weird porn shop and bought a…'

The game meant one thing: we had hours of driving ahead of us.

I looked out at the mountains. 'The Flinders Ranges?' I said, more to myself, eying jagged peaks soaring into ultra-white clouds against a sky so glossy blue it looked unreal, like children's wallpaper. Okay, the location had changed but my plans didn't need to.

'Are you playing or what?' asked Steve, looking at me with irritation.

I sat up more. I wasn't in the mood for an argument.

We'd made up this A–Z memory game while travelling that endless Stuart Highway through the Northern Territory. Memory games made sense when you a have two-lane road that stretches like a ruler for thousands of miles. You really don't want to fall asleep while a six-carriage road train is hurtling your way.

'You start,' I said.

'Okay, me-go-first.' He was sounding like a ten-year-old. 'I went to the weird porn shop and bought an anal vibrator.' A very inappropriate ten-year-old!

I looked at him. 'I'm pretty sure that exists. Our toys have to be made-up and let's make them really messed up.' Well, he wanted to stay awake.

It would be about ten minutes till Steve came up with 'alligator butt plugs' and another four hours until we turned off the bitumen. And we were in for one hellish ride along the roughest dirt roads I had ever experienced. The Bus was not built for off-road and would shit itself bigtime. I'd rejoice at that if nothing else.

# Dirt Road to Amirda

'How much of this road have we got left?' I asked as we crawled over uneven bumpy terrain at a snail's pace.

'About thirty Ks,' was the answer.

My mouth opened. Nothing but air came out. Eventually, I said, 'Well, at least tell me where we're going.'

'Okay,' he said as we dipped into a crater and crockery rattled about in the cupboards behind us.

The upshot was that the job in the Adelaide Hills had already been filled but the owners needed someone to caretake one of their stations in the north where – and this should have told Steve something – they were struggling to get someone. They were even thinking of destocking because of the six-year-long drought, even harsher the last three years. There was little saltbush for the sheep to feed on and the owner couldn't keep bringing bales of hay and feed from Adelaide – too expensive and impractical. If they did destock, then Steve would be the last caretaker for a while, and the station would close indefinitely.

While Steve was filling me in on the sheep station gig, I would occasionally let out a scream, 'Watch out!' as a roo bounded in front of us or an emu ran out of the way.

The further in we went, the denser the bush and trees got.

'How remote is this place?'

Steve didn't answer, but chewed on his lip. I was growing more and more angry at not being consulted about this move.

On we went, not passing a shop or house – nothing but roads and creeks and mountains, never-ending mountains that seemed to be closing in around us.

Then that sound you never want to hear came. It's the strange noise your tyre makes when it's blown: flip-flap-flop, over and over.

Steve brought the Bus to a stop. He opened the door, stuck his head out and growled a long drawn-out, 'Farrrrrrck.'

The heat was oppressive outside, like a hair dryer blowing in your face. Something white caught my eye. I looked closer. It was a spine, bleached white, belonging to what looked like a kangaroo. It still had bits of grey fur attached. There was another carcass further along, with feathers – an emu?

'You going to help or just stand there?' said Steve, kneeling by the shredded tyre.

I went over. 'What do you need?' I asked.

'I'll let you know,' he said with a sneer.

Steve wasn't good under pressure, but neither was my father, whom I loved dearly. I often wonder whether I married Steve because he reminded me of my dad. Trouble is, I'm not the daughter in this relationship but the wife, and Steve doesn't feel bad about behaving like an arsehole to me.

I felt that it would be easy to end up a carcass like the roos and emus in this dry oppressive heat. Hopefully, the carcasses weren't an omen and I'd live to tell the tale of my outback adventure. Although, the way Steve was sweating and turning scarlet, it looked like he might not survive this wheel change. I kept my fingers crossed.

Soon we were rattling our way through creeks and long stretches of white dirt road, if road you could call it. The dramatic mountains now surrounded us. They were spectacular to look at – different formations of peaks and edges, configurations of colossal size: some were a sequence of peach-like mounds looking like rows of Rubenesque bottoms set in gigantic relief. The colours too reminded me of pale peachy fruits, I guess pale because they were starved of water, Australia being in drought. Other mountains had rock formations running along the top like a castle fortress. And just visible criss-crossing this surreal landscape were fences, reminding me that it wasn't a fantasy land but farming country.

'Is this all the Flinders Ranges?' I asked.

'I. Have. No. Fucking. Idea,' spat Steve, wrestling with the oversized steering wheel as he navigated another set of potholes.

I looked out the window. The cabin fever was getting dangerous and I knew to shut up. But his struggle was giving me the giggles. My face started twitching. I prayed Steve wouldn't notice.

We dipped and tilted, getting jolted nearly out of our seats at one point – crockery in the back was smashing out of the cupboards now and the cabin rang with Steve's expletives. But moments later, we were on smoother track and Steve breathed easier. As did I.

'There! Look, some sheep,' I said, pointing excitedly at a sloping 'meadow' halfway down a mountain side – there was no green grass. Some sheep had black heads and shoulders, others were all white, and they were white. 'How is it these sheep look so white?' I asked. The sheep we had seen before looked positively dirty brown.

Steve didn't answer and was scowling. He didn't appear to hear me. Soon we were seeing more and more sheep. Some had fur dangling off their backs like they had been abandoned mid-shear. I didn't ask Steve about why that might be.

We began driving past wells and troughs, and those iconic Southern Cross windmills, their sails whirring in the wind.

'Wow, this place is stunning,' I blurted out, suddenly feeling excited and happy.

Steve looked over and his frown cleared up. He ran a hand over my knee and said, 'See, stick with me. Told you it would be good.'

I breathed out with relief. I needed Steve to be in a good mood.

So this was a sheep station in and among mountains. Not what I'd imagined an outback sheep station to be. I had in mind big, flat, open plains. This was much nicer. Nice? An insipid word for such scenery. Whatever, I was going to be Outback Heidi. I could hear the cowbells already. Okay, it was isolated, but there would be people who came to work on the farm, or workers and their families who lived on it, right? And I just knew a village must be around the corner. Maybe one with an old telegraph station. Anything faraway in Australia seems to have a disused telegraph station with a tea room for the public.

'Do other people work on the station?' I asked.

'Not sure what's there.'

'What's that?' I pointed to some movement in the trees that lined a creek.

Before Steve could answer, horses came into view. They were cinnamon brown with white strips down their faces. They were beautiful. Then, like something out of a movie, an Aboriginal guy on horseback emerged from the creek and rode ahead of the horses. As he came closer, I saw there was a child on the saddle with him. I waved and the cute kid waved back. The guy touched the rim of his hat at us and continued on. He was handsome. The smile on his face had a hint of mischief and seemed to suggest a smile at our expense, but perhaps I'm looking back with the filter of hindsight.

The Bus skidded in a stony creek and Steve had to rev the engine to stop us from getting bogged in the shale of pebbles. The horses bolted, disappearing into another part of the winding creek.

Before I could finish my 'How cool was that scene?' we came to a three-way sign where there was a sharp right turn. The arrow pointing straight ahead said Amirda. The road disappeared into shimmering heat vapours.

'Amirda, that's where we're going,' said Steve, crossing a cattle grid with fencing either side.

The other signs pointed to places called Urdlu and somewhere that began with the letter K. We followed the arrow towards the mirages. There were sheep everywhere now – mostly plain white, herds of goats too, some with mighty big horns, like real billy goat gruffs.

I looked back at the sign and said, 'Amirda. Ew, sounds like a murder.'

Steve looked at me. 'Trust you to think of that.'

'It sounds like a murder, end of – that's not a "trust you" thing.' I made the inverted comma signs at him with my fingers. He hates when I do that. I could get away with irking him now.

We drove for another ten K. Eventually, just when I was giving up hope of ever getting anywhere, we crossed the last cattle grid and were limping to the homestead with yet another burst tyre. The last creek we crossed landed us right at the homestead. The noise of the bus disturbed what looked like a hundred white cockatoos. They screeched at each other and flew up to the highest branches of further trees. Steve pointed to some kangaroos bounding off in the distance.

'This place is a nature reserve,' I said, seeing a large eagle take flight in the distance. I was looking around for signs of human life. I could only see sheep.

Then I saw the house or, rather, the veranda that surrounded it. Looked like something out of the wild west. I wouldn't have been surprised to see ole Grandpa on it, wearing chaps and a gun holster, with spurs on his boots, chewing tobacco. Behind him would be his son, the Duke, dressed the same, and the lady of the house might be called Belle Star. She was wearing long brown culottes and had her rifle at the ready to shoot rabbits or us trespassers.

In front of the homestead was a long white sign with black lettering, reading 'IRDA'. The initial AM was covered by the drooping leaves of a large tree. A gust of wind blew the branches sideways, revealing the full Amirda sign.

'Well, this is us for the next three months,' said Steve, bringing the Bus to a stop.

I pulled back the curtain behind us, and had a good look in the back. It was a mess. 'The kitchen sink tap is now in the sink,' I said with a groan.

'Are you deliberately trying to piss me off?' was Steve's response to my pointing out an inescapable fact.

I looked at him with my face screwed up.

He put a hand to his head and said, 'Sorry, sorry, just had a bad drive. I'll be all right. Just give me a minute.' He squeezed my knee just a little too tight.

I opened the door and stepped out. I was hoping a friendly sheep dog might come bounding over… But what if it were a guard dog? I took a step back, keeping close to the Bus. I looked around. The place looked like a village, there were so many buildings. No dog came into view. There was nothing but flies and I had to constantly fan my face.

Everywhere was very quiet. Even the cockatoos had shut up. It was too quiet and my spirits were sinking. Yet the place was busy-looking. There were lots of vehicles sitting under carports, and there were outhouses, and garages with motorbikes in, but no sign of life.

'Look, that's a petrol pump,' I said. 'This place has its own gas station.' I started walking over to it.

'Yeah, think that's pretty standard for outback stations,' said Steve. His voice was back to normal, to nice mode.

I relaxed. He too was looking around with his brow knitted.

When we reached the sole-pump gas station, I said, 'Wonder if we can get a Chiko roll?'

I walked towards the pump and trod on a sheet of corrugated metal. There were a few such sheets about.

The wind got up again and a banging noise caught our attention. We looked over to a building missing some of its side panels. This was probably where the sheet metal had come from. Another sheet on the roof, like the one I'd stepped on, was flapping, causing the banging noise. Bit by bit, the shed was getting blown apart.

'Hope I'm not in the way when the next one rips off,' I said, now seeing more sheet metal strewn around the grounds of what was clearly a very empty property in terms of human life. Flies, just flies for company.

Steve walked over to have a look at the falling-apart shed. It was packed with rusty junk – old chairs, ancient pots of paint, old brooms, bedsteads, speckled mirrors – the life of yesteryears, full of shit basically.

'And a mummified roo,' I said. I went further in but had to walk out again because of the stifling, weird smell, no doubt caused by that roo. I had a thought. 'Hey, it's gone five. Maybe everyone has knocked off for the day.' Then I was looking at a large building on stilts that ran alongside the creek. A door at the top of a flight of steps said woolshed. 'Steve, maybe there are people in there.' I pointed at the woolshed.

Steve strode over. I let him go up and open the door. The draping cobwebs he had to fight his way through, Indiana Jones style, announced there was no one in there. I stepped in and saw bits of wool strewn across the slatted wooden floors, the hanging shears full of cobwebs, part of a fleece on a table – it gave me a creepy feeling, like one day the workforce had downed tools and walked out, never to be seen again.

I turned to Steve and said, 'There's no one here, I mean anywhere on this property, is there?'

Steve didn't answer. He was walking out of the building, perhaps to get some air.

I said, following him out, 'Is the owner even meeting us?'

From the foot of the steps, Steve gave me a weak smile and raised eyebrows, putting his hand on his hips. He said nothing.

'What is it?' I asked, walking down to meet him, dreading his reply.

'The owner is coming to meet us.' Steve looked at his watch. 'About now, I should say.' Then he said, 'But the guy doesn't live here. It will be just us.' He waved away flies from his mouth with an up and down and sideways palm, like the pope giving a benediction. I hadn't taken it in when Steve had said, 'They can't get anyone to caretake out there.'

Someone should have said to me, 'What part of caretake don't you understand?' Of course, it was just us. If anyone worked here, there wouldn't be falling-down wrecks of sheds. I felt my stomach contract with fear.

## Meeting the Aussie Landed Gentry

I didn't get a chance to process the bad news and think too much about how we could be like that couple in Stephen King's The Shining, where the man turns psycho on his wife while he's caretaking the empty desolate hotel.

The sound of a vehicle, along with plumes of dust, signalled the arrival of someone.

Steve said, 'And here he comes.'

We watched the car come to a halt next to us. It was a shiny beast of a ute encased in chrome bull-bars that looked strong enough to repel a herd of rhinoceros. It was pulling a trailer full of boxes, gas cylinders, car tyres and much more besides. A darkened window came down on the ute, and we were looking at a beaming smile under a large cowboy hat with a dip at its top you could carry eggs in. His teeth were clogged with food debris, and judging by the amount of empty wrappers on the dashboard, he had snacked his way here. The ute door opened and he stepped out, shedding crumbs everywhere. I stared at his bare feet poking out of shredded jeans. He reached in the door and pulled out a beer. Then he wiped a free hand on his blue shirt, smearing grease on it. I saw a bag of chicken on the passenger seat. I pictured him grabbing handfuls of it while he was driving. He thrust out his hand for Steve to shake, and then for me. I was relieved not to find his palm greasy.

'I'm El Cid. Nice to meet you both finally. How you going?'

His name wasn't El Cid, but that's what I came to call him. For all his unkempt appearance, he was epic, like something out of legend. That is how I came to feel.

I could have kicked myself when I said, 'How do you do, sir.'

Steve looked at me with his face slightly screwed up. He seemed to be saying, 'Why don't you curtsey too?'

El Cid stood back theatrically. 'Sir,' he mocked. 'Do I look like a black fella with a gun?'

I didn't get the reference or joke, but I didn't need to. His laughing, booming voice was welcome in that eerie, deserted place.

We talked a little about how we found the place okay, and then Cid said, 'And you're a writer, Loraine.' He nodded at me, smiling as if encouraging me to say more about it.

I was taken aback, and involuntarily looked at Steve. He had told him that?

'Yeah, I've had a little success,' I said, unsure what to say about my Ashgate book on George Orwell. It was still in print but not making any real headway in Orwell studies, which bothered me, understandably.

'We've got a good library in there.' He nodded towards the house. 'Got books about Amirda too. Have a good read in your downtime.' He began telling us about his collection but all I could think about was his emphasis on the word 'downtime'. Did he expect that I would be working?

'C'mon, I'll take you up to the shed, show you the working heart of Amirda,' he said.

For a second, I thought he might be taking us to the junk shed with the dead roo and I was wondering why, but when we approached what looked like a massive aeroplane hangar, I saw my mistake.

Cid had to put his shoulder to the corrugated slide door to make it move. He explained that the rollers needed greasing. 'Job for you already, Steve,' he said, winking at me.

The door made a screechy grating sound just like the giant iron statues do when they come to life in Jason and the Argonauts. It was freaky. When the door was finally rolled all the way open, I half expected to see a Boeing 747 parked inside.

What was in there was difficult to make out because it was all thick with red dust and looked like some lost city in need of excavation.

Cid said to me, 'D'ya drink piss, miss?'

'Sorry?' Was 'piss' vinegar – did I have a sour look?

When he pulled open a fridge revealing a stack of cold beer (ice clouds on the bottles said the fridge was on), his meaning was clear. He pulled two out and handed one to each of us. 'There should be stubby holders around,' he said, and sure enough, there were, dusty ones.

Cid sat down on a milk crate and pulled some boots towards him. He shook them upside down and put them on – still with no socks. 'Your van doesn't look too happy,' he said, standing up.

'Nothing that can't be fixed,' said Steve.

'We saw some beautiful horses,' I chipped in.

He darted me a look, and said, 'The brumbies, where were they?'

Steve said, 'Out by the turn-off to Urdlu and Kuren…er…'

'Kurra Weena. Before the grid or after?' His face clouded over.

'The horses were before the grid,' said Steve.

I was amazed he could remember.

This cleared up Cid's frown and he said, 'That's all right then.'

'Are the horses a problem?' I asked.

'They are if they take my water.' He sniffed and guzzled down his beer.

I asked him if they were wild and he said, 'They are and they're not. They belong to the black fellas at Urdlu, and as long as they keep them there, I don't have a problem. Water's scarce with the drought.'

'There was an Aboriginal guy on horseback too. He had a little boy with him.'

Cid brightened, 'Ah, yeah. Did he say g'day?'

'He did, well, he gave us a touch of his hat –'

Stop right there. I need to make a correction. Because, you know what, if I'm going to tell 'my truth', I should cut out the BS about Aboriginals on horseback. We saw those horses, but there was no one riding any horse. The guy we came across was in a beat-up old car, and he didn't touch his hat to us, because he wasn't wearing one. He gave us a cold stare. He did have a nice little kid next to him, though, who did wave. Why did I lie? I guess because that's what I wanted to see.

Okay, from now on, although I will change place names and people's names for all the usual reasons, I won't lie about what happened, no matter how much I'm tempted.

Now, where was I? Talking about the horses we had seen.

I asked El Cid if he used horses to muster the sheep into pens for sheering. I'd seen plenty of ranchers on horseback doing musters on TV documentaries.

'Nope, don't ride. Got thrown from a horse when I was five and never got back on. It's better on bikes anyways.'

'What's at Koro Weeny?' Steve asked.

'Kuraa Weena,' said Cid with a hint of impatience. 'It's a nature park, a bit of bush-camping. They got a rifle range, you get some goat-shooters going, motocross too.'

There was too much talk of shooting for my liking. Was that why Cid didn't have dogs around? Was he worried about them getting shot?

'Do you use working dogs at all?' I asked. 'With the sheep?'

'Mongrels, dogs, more trouble than they're worth,' he said, looking angry, and said something about needing a part from his car.

As he walked out of the shed, I made a note to self: don't mention working dogs.

While he was gone, Steve didn't say a word but looked around the hanger at the packed shelves and the different equipment. His head was on a swivel like he was in awe of the workshop and didn't know what to focus on.

Cid came back and, tapping a ute that was parked under a hoist, I hadn't noticed before, said, 'Got a part for the clutch. Here, Steve,' he said, nodding at the base of the hoist, 'you push those levers under the car, can you? We'll get her up and oil her nipples first.' He laughed.

For a minute, I was appalled at the grubby language and rolled my eyes, but it turns out he was using correct terminology – Steve would be forever greasing nipples on vehicle chassis.

I stepped right out of the way as the ute went up into the air, the hoist making alarming clunking noises as the vehicle got lifted in stages. For the next half an hour, we watched Cid work on the ute –

it was clear he knew what he was doing as he extracted one part and replaced it with another. He unplugged wires, blew at them or wiped them and put them back into place. His big blue shirt got covered in black oil and, by the time the car was done, he looked like a mechanic.

More beers in hand, we walked down to a trough where there were sheep gathered. Many were sitting under trees or just milling around. Some of them had their fleeces hanging off.

'How come the fleeces are hanging off like that?' I asked Cid. 'Or didn't the shearers finish them off?'

'It's the heat. They're shedding their winter coat still,' he said.

'They shed wool and get shorn as well?' I queried, hoping my questions weren't silly.

'No shearers needed with dorpers. We don't use the wool,' he said, looking around as if surveying the land. 'Haven't told your wife about dorpers, Steve?'

He thinks Steve communicates with me, I thought. Bleating made me turn around. It was coming from two little lambs trying to get at their mother's teats.

'Aw, those lambs are so cute. She's had twins,' I said quietly.

Cid explained that dorpers usually have twins, and sometimes even three. He said they were good mums too.

'They birth all year round, right?' said Steve.

'That's exactly right,' said Cid, seeming to nod with satisfaction.

'But why don't you want the wool?' I asked, getting more confused about what the hell his sheep were for.

'Dorper sheep are bred for meat, not wool. They shed when it gets too thick, so don't need to shear them. Merinos got all the wool, and I haven't had merinos on Amirda since the wool crash. That's going on twenty year.'

The woolshed wouldn't be coming back to life then. Another blow to my romantic dreams of muscly shearers whistling while they work.

He added, 'Merinos and shearers are more trouble than they're worth.'

I hadn't known him for half an hour but already, I knew three of his most unfavourite things: horses, working dogs and sheep-shearers. Cid was like Maria's Sound of Music in the negative.

The trough was full of green slime.

'Steve, that's your first job tomorrow, to get the waters potable. Imagine that in your coffee.'

Steve and I took a closer look at the green slime right through the trough.

'Not nice. You coming out tomorrow, miss?' asked Cid.

I told him I would certainly be going on the water run. I smiled at the idea that he thought I would remain behind on my own in the ghost town.

Then he said to Steve, 'You might want to give me a hand to get the chucks out of the trailer and into the hen house. My bad. They'll be hot as in those boxes.'

With a smelly chuck-in-a-box, I followed Cid around to the back of the house. In a fenced-off space overgrown with what turned out to be bamboo grasses was the sorry chuck shed. I put the box over the fence. God only knew what was under all that growth. I winced when I saw chicken feet sticking out of some hay. I saw something move – a chicken was alive in there? I stared at the moving thing – what was that? Then I saw its head. It was a snake! I screamed and pointed.

Cid said calmly, 'Yeah, there's a few snakes around so keep ya boots on and you'll be right.'

You'll be right – I'd be very far from right.

## Is that Halloween Wallpaper?

The veranda around the house that I had admired from afar was in disrepair. Great chunks of the floor had fallen away at the edges and parts of the railing were missing support poles or just missing altogether.

Cid, nodding at the house, said, 'Needs a bit of work, I know. You any good at masonry, Steve?'

That's when I noticed great cracks along the structure of the bricks. Cid explained that the limestone foundations of the house were being undermined by the water table running underneath. The German architects had built too close to it.

'No, sorry,' was Steve's firm reply. 'Done a bit of reno but not with stone.'

I rested my hand on a chair and Steve said, 'Get your hand off there.'

I did. He had spotted a red-back nest of egg sacs on the backrest. He picked up a broom leaning on the wall of the veranda and began clearing the webs from chairs around the outdoor table.

'Come on, we'll go inside,' said Cid, taking off his boots.

As I was putting my boots against the wall, I saw something move. I didn't want to look, I knew what it was going to be, and if it was a snake, we were getting the hell out of the place. But maybe it was just a – holy sweet crap, the thing came into view from behind some crates. It was a snake twice as big as the one in the chicken coop.

Before I could get the words out, it was disappearing around the corner – a long brown snake, that was an eastern brown. 'Snake,' I cried, pointing at the wall.

Cid laughed, saying, 'They won't come near you, and if they do…' He grabbed a spade from I don't know where and said, '…you chop it with this.'

He made to go at me with the spade and I stumbled back, knocking over a crate of empty beer bottles.

Steve started picking them up and I hissed in his ear, 'No way are we staying.'

He said through a side crack in his mouth, 'It'll be fine.'

I was so freaked out about what I might step on, bump into, or disturb that I didn't pay much attention to what Cid said as we followed him into and through his Addams Family home. Our feet crunched on stuff, mostly sand that was blowing in from the open or cracked windows. This main entrance was a kind of office, somewhat antiquated with its very big computers. It obviously hadn't been used since the last century. There was a montage of pictures around and maps. The pictures looked like his children and wife.

I pointed at it and said, 'This your family, Cid?'

'Yeah, that's the missus, and the kids when they were small. Bit more grown up now.'

'How old are your children now?' I asked.

To that he said, 'What's this, quiz night?'

I guess I had to stop with the questions. We went from room to room where wool carpets had been eaten threadbare by moths. There was a dining room with his stern-looking ancestors hung on the walls – sepia pictures of people who didn't smile for the camera as we have to now. A serious young man dressed in a three-piece suit with a stiff collar looked out at us from his staged background. It looked like El Cid a hundred years ago. His eyes were exactly the same. There were more of the same boy in other photos along with women in long frilly dresses.

'Who's that?' I asked Cid, pointing at the boy who looked like him.

'It's my grandpa,' he said.

The dark green wallpaper that the pictures hung from looked like it hadn't been changed since the 1930s (that turned out to be the case). The snooker room next to it was a sad affair – the felt on the table was all torn up and didn't have a dust cover. Some rooms had large goat heads on the walls which had cobwebs going from horn to horn, like rows of ghostly hammocks. I noticed a cane chair and imagined granny's skeleton rocking in it.

Cid's phone rang. He said, looking at the screen, 'My manager.' He left the room. Seconds later, he was shouting down the phone, 'Fucking mole, silly lazy cunt.'

'He seems to be having staff problems,' I said.

Steve didn't answer but said, 'Look at this.'

He was pointing at a framed newspaper clipping on a side table. It was a picture of Cid's wife dressed like an Irwin in green ranger clothes and wearing a hat like Cid's. She was surrounded by women and children in a school hall. The children were giving her a placard which read, 'Thank You for Your Bushfire Support.' I was right, she was a country woman, active on behalf of her community.

El Cid came back and resumed his tour. Next, the library. It was dusty but looked well-preserved, apart from all the cracks that had torn the wallpaper – more signs the house was tilting. He showed us the books on Amirda that various relatives had produced. They were full of old photographs, some of Cid when he was a boy. I particularly liked one of little Cid, sat on the woolshed floor, pulling at a fleece. There were many pages giving diagrams of bores and wells, showing depths and other dimensions.

'Some of these bores are overdue for a clean, Steve. You'll help with me with that.'

Steve agreed with enthusiasm – that is, with the briefest nod. We went back to the kitchen, which was just off the office entrance. It was filthy. The cooker top was thick with burnt overspills. I dreaded to think what the inside of the oven looked like. Cid opened a cupboard and I took a sharp intake of breath when I saw a freaky thickset forest of –

'What is that?' I asked, stepping closer to what looked like an overgrowth of white roots systems like some alien invasion. I was starting to feel strange, awful; a memory was being triggered. I had seen this horror show before, in my own home, when Mum was gone for all that time.

'Sorry, looks like someone left potatoes on that shelf,' said Cid, looking apologetic, but not for long.

'I'll get you to clean that up, Steve,' was my closing remark walking away.

There would be flour crawling with weevils, and heaven only knew what was being cultivated in the fridge Cid had just opened, botulism in the yoghurt perhaps, if those clouded pots were any indication. Cid apologised again and said the place had been neglected, and the last people had upped and left not giving any notice. It was clear the whole kitchen needed an overhaul if we were going to stay, but it was a job for someone with a strong stomach and capable of tough scrubbing – Steve.

We continued our tour. I yelped when, on entering the sitting room, I saw huntsman spiders on the walls, some as big as your hand. It was like a room decorated with Halloween wallpaper.

Cid said, 'They won't bite you.'

We were shown to our bedroom. It was an old sitting room with a brick inglenook that had not seen a fire in decades, I was guessing. I could already see without having to look closely that there were mouse and gecko droppings on the sills and in the fireplace. And if it's true that people have spiders crawl into their open mouths at night, this was the place for it. Cid told us where we could find fresh sheets. And to my relief they were clean.

There was a bathroom across the hallway that was for our sole use. It needed a thorough clean, like everything else. It was no surprise that the plumbing wasn't working.

After a few unsuccessful flushes of the toilet and tinkering with the cistern, Cid said, 'Can you go up to the shed, Steve and get…' Cid reeled off the spanners and other tools that he wanted to fix the toilet. 'Can't have you pissing in the wind, eh?' he said, then shouted after Steve, 'Here, I'll come with you.'

I noticed the shower had a sand-glass egg timer on a shelf. The three-minute shower had followed us here. The spa bath was out then, even if I could get the stains out! My shoulders sagged. Then I noticed there were jumping things – crickets. There were crickets all over the bathroom. I got out as quick as I could.

When Cid had got the toilet flushing – he really was a whizz with the tools – he asked us to come and get some meat and groceries out of his car fridge. 'We'll have a barbecue for tea, will we?' he said, heading out.

The sun was setting beyond the creek and the tops of the trees were a silhouette of black set against hues of pink and orange, a dazzling live painting that literally stopped us in our tracks, at least it did me and Steve. Cid marched on.

Cid's car was loaded with grocery bags, sacks of vegetables, all sorts. While he and Steve grappled with offloading the car fridge, I started taking in the shopping.

When I commented on how much food there was, Cid said, 'We didn't want you to starve.'

When the car was emptied it became clear that it was going to be my job to clean out the fridge and freezer after all, and the dreaded potato-forest cupboard. Cid asked Steve to help him with a few jobs, and he wanted to show him this and that.

It was a good thing that I didn't have time to think. I got bin liners from the cockroach infestation under the sink and got to work. I used one bin liner as a glove to sweep out the colonies of unidentifiable food stuffs. The other liner caught the exploding rotten potatoes and their snapping spitting roots. It was traumatic, triggering confronting memories of a like experience back home when I was a veritable Cinderella and my brothers the 'ugly sisters' watching me doing all the housework while they lounged around. But, as then, I got the job done. I filled the bin bag and several more. Alas, this was no time for recycling – the rubbish would burn. Once I had wiped up the left-behind mouldy deposits, it was hey presto, I could put the groceries away.

Cid told us that his missus had ordered our supplies online. She had been generous. The fridge ended up looking like a fruit and veg stall at harvest festival.

Before we could have our evening meal, we had to clean up the barbecue plate – the river of congealed grease was something else. While Steve had that nice job, I set to a thorough brush-down of the red-back table and chairs, then got a salad bowl together to go with the copious amounts of meat Cid had ready to sizzle on the barbie for tea. Tea! No genteel 'supper' or dinner, just tea. I liked that. I still like the way Aussies aren't snobby about meals or anything else much no matter what their social status.

At tea, I saw Cid had no time for the delicacies of dabbing one's mouth with a napkin. I smiled at the English obsession with table manners or, rather, I smiled at the idea that Cid would never be appalled by someone calling a napkin a serviette. This lord of the manor wiped his fingers on his shirt and his mouth on the back of his hand. He was like some medieval king who pleased himself. At least he carried a cotton hanky for his nose, which seemed always in need of blowing.

However, like a king, he didn't do cleaning. While Cid retired to the veranda to make calls, Steve and I washed up. Cid waved us a goodnight around nine o'clock, and we got to work on cleaning our bathroom and bedroom.

When we were finally in bed, Steve said, taking my hand in his, as we lay staring at the cobwebs on the ceiling we'd missed, 'I think we'll be all right in this place, don't you?'

'I'll give it a go, Steve,' I said, giving his hand a squeeze back.

To my surprise, Steve was lightly snoring within minutes. Of course, he'd been driving all day as well as all the work. It was almost a full moon and thanks to a cloudless sky the room was lit with a silver light illuminating the antique furniture around the room which I had given a dust. I thought about my Orwell book and my abandoned career as a promising academic. It was fear, was it not, that made me quit my lecturing job at Liverpool University? Or was it just too much work? I was almost anorexic, which made me look good in my professor's jacket up on that podium, but the knots in my stomach made my life unbearable. How scared I was of that sea of student faces, dreading a question I couldn't answer. Always afraid, anxious. Yet what had changed?

I looked out into the creek, a ghostlike woodland of white gumtrees under the moon's light. Write that thriller, make it good, make it the best it can be, and you will be published again only with much more success, and all your other books will have life again. Yes, that was it – I would write myself into a new start, I thought, as my eyes closed with relief.

I was surprised when I opened my eyes to find it was morning. Steve was awake on his phone, as usual. I looked out of the dirty window and knew I didn't want to stay in the creepy house, for all our cleaning. I needed a place to write, somewhere I wouldn't be distracted by fear of isolation when left alone. We had to get back on the road, or get to Adelaide as planned.

'I'm not sure I'm going to be able to last in this place,' I said, turning to Steve.

He was playing Candy Crush. Without taking his eyes of the screen, he said, 'You got us into this, remember, so at least give it three months. I'm not messing this guy around because you're afraid of spiders.'

I felt tears coming – I hated this kind of coldness from him, and yes, this kind of pathetic reaction by me. I steeled myself and was determined to be more balanced and explain why I wanted to get away because the place was too weird, but I sank inside and just hated him. Fine, I thought, if I had to get away, I would simply drive off in one of those vehicles outside. No need for more arguments or having him shove his face in mine, or worse… I was free to leave of my own free will, right?

# The Water Run

The smell of bacon made Steve and me jump out of bed.

'He's got breakfast on,' said Steve, struggling with his shorts.

I wondered how I was going to eat so early in the morning. Yet we were going to be out all day on the water run, and so I'd better make the effort.

'Can you get some eggs from the chuck house, one of you?' asked Cid as we stepped onto the veranda.

I volunteered, and Cid pointed to some wellies I could wear.

When I reached the chickens, I heard El Cid on his phone – clearly, he had left the barbecue and come to the other end of the veranda to take his call – so Steve couldn't listen in? He was f-ing, c-ing, and lazy-mole-ing this and that again. I knew now that he had a cattle station in Broken Hill (I was loving the names) just over the border in New South Wales. His manager was having problems with the staff there, he'd told us, although not about what. I wondered what the hell was going wrong to cause the manager guy so much grief. Perhaps cattle were different to sheep. I would get to find out just how.

After breakfast, we stayed in the office to look at maps of the area, and specifically Amirda, which showed the property's land in detail. I was astonished to learn that Amirda sat on 2,000 square kilometres. To put that into perspective, Snowdonia in Wales is 2,130 square kilometres. The guy owned the equivalent of a county or national park with just one house on it, and he didn't even live there.

He pointed out a creek and said, 'There's ancient cave paintings here. I'll take you to see them sometime.'

I wondered about the Aboriginals who had once lived in the area. There was a long-forgotten history here. Perhaps Cid didn't even know what it was. I suspected it was not in those family books on the making of Amirda.

We moved to another wall, and another larger map. This one was of the surrounding five stations. Looking at the map and its scale, it felt like Amirda was a county in England, an empty one. How England might have looked over 4,000 years ago. In fact, when you looked at the surrounding stations, this part of the Flinders Ranges was like the whole United Kingdom, but inhabited by a handful of families. Yes, think of the British Isles well before it was conquered by the Romans. Miles upon miles of unspoilt hills and meadows, only instead of being criss-crossed with rivers and willow trees, this had a zillion dry creeks lined with gum trees. It didn't do to think of what the Aboriginal map might have looked like then, but history had gone this way, Cid's way.

By six thirty, after cleaning the Amirda trough by the house, we were heading out. My back was already reeling from the rigours of brushing and we had seventeen more troughs to go! Cid was in the driving seat of the work ute. Steve was holding a map to follow the water-run route. I was squashed in the middle and would spend an entire day trying to keep my knee away from Cid's hand as he changed gears, which seemed to be constantly along the bumpy terrain, plus he was in and out of four-wheel drive.

The first trough to clean was Camel-foe. My names for the troughs rhymed with the actual names so as not to get confused when the originals were referred to. At Camel-foe, we disturbed the sheep at their morning drink. They tripped over each other and over the trough to escape us. Steve went to get out when we stopped but Cid told him to wait. A lamb had got separated from its mother and it was panicking. It was ramming into the fence trying to bust its way out – not realising it only had to turn and run the other way to escape.

'It will headbutt itself to death if you go near it,' said Cid, scratching his head under his large hat.

The mother came a little closer and the lamb did turn, thankfully scampering away.

'That's a good mother,' said Cid. 'Some of 'em just go.'

I was about to remind him that he said dorpers made for good mothers, but clearly there were exceptions just like in the human world.

This trough was supplied by a tank that got its water from a bore deep underground. A Southern Cross windmill brought the water up from the bore – the wind had to keep blowing for the windmill to work.

As Steve got the brushes out to clean the slime from the trough, Cid was on his phone again, shouting, 'F\*\*king useless mole, f\*\*king c\*nt…'

I had visions of angry cattle trampling down fences and trashing the feeder stations and troughs with a red-faced manager chasing after them, scratching his hot head under an oversized cowboy hat.

Travelling around Amirda was like Jurassic Park to me in scale and wonders. The single track we followed was like the monorail track in the movie. But instead of a herd of diplodocus and brachiosaurus or a pack of velociraptors, it was emus with tall chicks that crossed our path and eagles that flew overhead, or it was well-camouflaged kangaroos that sprang out from the scrub and hopped away or fled from a trough when we drove close. There were many stockyards, empty of sheep, some in disrepair, and many overgrown with weeds and unwanted bushes.

'They'll have to come out, come muster,' said Cid.

Steve nodded. I groaned inwardly. But weeding would be a doddle compared to the horrors that awaited us in those yards. I had no idea of the chaos that would unfold in those yards at mustering: apocalyptic scenes amidst clouds of blinding dust and heated confusion as man and sheep became blurred. But for now, they were peaceful sunny places.

Sadly, along the fence lines, there was the occasional dead roo that had got its legs caught trying to jump a fence. Many had their eyes pecked out, and one could only hope they hadn't had to last too long in that trapped position before death released them.

I asked Cid if he ate kangaroo.

His reply, 'Do I look like a black fella?' Ditto with emus.

It seemed that the white fellas brought in the hoofed animal and would only eat them, or this white fella at any rate.

Lots of water tanks had their share of problems. One was overflowing because the float had popped a seal. That was a half-hour job – just finding the right float took an age (they all have different fittings). At another watering hole, some pipes had leaks underground and needed digging up. Cid's phone was ringing constantly when he could get a signal so Steve was having to do most of the digging. I was doing a lot of hanging around, mostly earwigging Cid's conversations.

As Steve was digging at the dry ground, I heard Cid saying, 'He did what?' Pause. 'Stupid mole.' Pause. 'He said what?' Pause. 'Fucking cunt.' Pause. 'What? I can't hear.' Pause. 'He said he couldn't do it? Fucking lazy mole cunt…' If his language sounds shocking as I write it, when spoken by El Cid it wasn't offensive somehow – it was rather funny.

When Cid got off the phone and came over, I said, 'Sorry, I couldn't help overhearing. Sounds like your manager is still having problems. Is it with someone over in Broken Hill?' I was hoping he might say a bit more than I'd got out of him the night before at our barbecue.

Steve rolled his eyes at me.

Cid scratched under his hat, where I could see sweat was gathering. He said, 'Yeah, she's got some staff issues, that's right.'

Oh, so it was a she. I suddenly saw a different picture – the cowboys weren't happy that a sheila was in charge of them!

I was about to say that I was sorry to hear this when he said, clapping his hands together, 'Anyway, enough about that, let's see Steve mend a pipe.'

Steve looked up from the hole he had dug, where water was spurting out. Cid got some iron tools from the ute and chucked them on the ground near Steve's feet. I could hear Steve swear under his breath as he picked up the mole grips, wiping his brow. Poor Steve, it was going to be a long hard day for him.

I was surprised and delighted to see that there was a natural spring on the land, and even in drought it still had water enough for a dip. Cid told Steve to always check that a sheep had not fallen in and drowned. I was pleased to see a water source we wouldn't have to maintain as much as looking at the spring as a swimming pool.

'Cool off in here whenever you like,' said Cid.

If it were not for the constant 'illegal' campers making use of that spring, we might well have utilised it more.

At one of the last paddocks, near the homestead called Afghan (named after the first cameleers), many dorpers were on the wrong side of the fence.

'There's a hole somewhere,' said Cid. 'Roos dig under the fence all the time.' He explained that Steve needed to get on the bike and do regular fence checks. The fence could usually be pulled back in place, and the hole filled in. 'Rocks are your friends here,' he assured Steve.

Steve nodded like he understood but I knew he'd be thinking, 'I'll work it out.' Just like he'd have to work out how to muster the sheep back into the paddock without it taking the entire day.

## Guns, Managers and Mistresses

The next morning was a case of déjà vu or Groundhog Day, as we woke up to the same scene: the hens clucking and Cid sizzling bacon and sausages, only this time he had moved into the kitchen and was cooking on an electric pot. It would be the last time Cid cooked breakfast, ever. He was talking on his phone, and as usual, he was f-ing and mole-c-ing. I didn't know whether to cough to let him know I was there. I wished I had when he whispered, 'Love you too,' into his phone.

I tried to step away quietly but banged into a chair.

He turned around, saw me, and said a hurried, 'Got to go,' into his phone. I didn't know where to look when he said a cheerful, 'Morning.'

Was it why he didn't show much interest in those photos of his wife and kids – he was having it on with the manager? Ah, maybe that's why she was having problems with her staff – she wasn't good at her job but was bonking the boss, so she couldn't get fired.

Steve came into the kitchen looking sleepy. My thoughts went back to Cid. Perhaps he and his wife lived separate love lives but stayed together for appearances' sake and for their children too.

'Got some bike tyres on the trailer there, Steve. You good at changing tyres?' asked Cid.

Steve said, 'I'll give it a go.' Jeez, such questions before he'd had a feed.

Cid must have sensed that Steve wasn't confident because he said to me, 'Can you take over breaky and chuck on a few eggs in a bit while I help Steve?' Then he said, 'Get you in practice.' He winked at me and said, 'You don't mind?'

'No, of course, I can do that,' I said. Cid was a master at putting people to work.

Half an hour later, when they hadn't come back, I went up to the shed. There was a lot of nice language coming from there. Cid was stood on a tyre that had crowbars sticking out between the wheel rim and the tyre. I went to get a closer look.

Cid shouted, 'Stand back. If the tyre pops, you'll get a fair whack in the head, if you don't lose it altogether.'

I didn't need telling twice and went back to the doorway. I noticed an open cabinet. It was full of rifles! 'Jesus, there's enough armoury in there to invade a small country,' I said, and wasn't joking.

Cid looked at the open gun cupboard. 'I'm taking some back.'

Oh my God, was he going to kill his wife so that he could be with the manager?

I left, saying, 'Your breakfast is getting cold.'

I was reeling now, at the thought of what could happen to Steve if one of those crowbars pinged out of the tyre rim, or what Cid might do with one of those rifles, and the fact that we had guns on the property for the taking – he wasn't taking them all away.

Then I stopped myself. This was the outback, all farmers had guns, I didn't need to panic. No, I needed to panic, guns everywhere, like Wolf Creek? It was murder central! If my nerves weren't shot enough (pun intended), I was halfway to the homestead when there was a clamour of slamming doors all around. A gust of violent wind nearly toppled me over and my eyes were blinded with grit.

I righted myself to hear Cid shouting, 'Close the windows. Dust storm coming.'

I ran in and started shutting windows and doors. Blasts of dust clouds were already blowing in and stinging my eyes again. The drama of it. The day hadn't even begun and I was emotionally drained.

The dust storm didn't last long, and, after a sorry-looking breakfast, we all went back outside.

Cid said, 'I'll head back south today, if that's okay with you guys.'

Steve and I looked at each other, our mouths open to say something. I went first. 'Why so soon?' He had meant to be staying the week.

'Ah, got cattle missing. Fences are down and didn't get put back up

–' he looked at me and grinned, 'If you can't trust someone to do it, better do it yourself, eh?'

Was he really going back to be with his mistress? Perhaps they'd just started their affair, hence the whispering of sweet nothings. No! This was Brokeback Mountain and Cid was only pretending that his manager was a she. Broken Hill, Brokeback Mountain – sounds alike. Yeah, my imagination was off again.

Cid looked at Steve. 'You'll be right, Steve. Sheep don't give too much trouble, eh?'

Steve assured him, I think with over confidence, that he would absolutely be all right. I wanted to say but I won't be.

'You might have a bit of company,' he said.

I brightened.

'Might be getting some campers in the creek.'

'Campers?' I asked. He didn't answer and I started to get anxious. 'Who are they?'

Flies were crawling over his lips and nose. They were trying to get into my mouth too. I smacked them away.

'Don't the flies get to you?' I asked, perhaps with too much irritation.

Steve's glance at me suggested rudeness on my part.

He said, 'I rub camel shit on the back of my neck and that keeps them away.'

I stared at him as he laughed at his own joke, allowing flies to come and go into his mouth like it was a hotel lobby. Did he no longer notice?

'So, about the campers,' I reminded him. 'Who are they?'

He shrugged and said, after spitting flies of his lip, 'Don't know. We got a tourism site on the Internet for outback camping. Take $30 if they don't hook up to the electricity. Charge them $50 a night if they do.'

'Do people have to register before coming? You know, do you take their passports or ID?'

He frowned at me. 'What for?'

My face must have clouded over.

He laughed at me and said, 'Why the long face? It's all good. No problems out here.'

But I wasn't happy at the thought of strangers camping with us. I was appalled that he was advertising this remote place on the Internet. So every man and his dog could come and see this place was open for the taking. Jesus, you could get anyone coming here.

Then I caught Cid looking at me with a little smile. He was joking! Maybe it was all a big joke at my expense. There would be no strangers camping and he wasn't even leaving – Steve had told him how jittery I was about being alone in the outback. He was winding up the nervous townie Pommie.

Not long afterwards, we watched him get back into his big shiny ute and drive off. Oh yes, he was most definitely leaving us, and Amirda was open for any Tom, Dick or hatchet-wielding Harry to visit.

We watched the clouds of dust swirling up behind his car as he raced away. I wanted to run after him and shout, 'Don't leave us here, alone!' I felt ill at the thought of being in the middle of absolutely nowhere by ourselves, or worse, with creepy travellers who could just rock up and help themselves to his gun cabinet. And instead of paying, maybe they'd just shoot us.

When his vehicle had disappeared out of sight, I stared at Steve and said, 'What have you tricked me into?'

His response took me by surprise when he picked me up and said, turning me around like I was some kid in its parent's arms, 'This is gonna be an adventure for us, baby.' He put me down and did a kind of dance. 'Tonight, let's have a bottle of wine to celebrate our new freedom. No "happy campers" to spoil our views, either.' He took my hand and led me to the Bus. 'We might just have two, hey?' He kissed me on the cheek, saying, 'And spend today uploading your funny animal pics to your socials, you love that.'

And just like that, I was caught up in his enthusiasm, and it was as if I was looking at someone new. Maybe this was the change I'd been hoping for – maybe there was something to 'me and Steve' after all. My mind raced with thoughts, not of flight, but of giving us both another go. I had been drawn down into a vortex of negativity in the Bus…too much close proximity had brought out the worst in him. Wow, could it be that I did have the man of my life? And so I was back on the wedded-bliss hamster wheel for a while, although the bliss was short-lived when Steve left me alone to go and mend that fence at Afghan and then turn his talents to mustering alone.

## Trying to Talk to My Mother

The next day, while Steve was in the shower, I went into the office and called my mother. It was about nine at night, her time. When she came into view, I could only see part of her head. Looked like she was pulling herself out of her seat. Since she's had a reclining chair, that's pretty much how every conversation begins.

'I'll be with you in a minute, let me turn down the tele,' she said.

While she got herself conversation-ready, I wondered what she would make of my new faraway adventure.

'So,' she began, with a squint, peering over my shoulder, 'you look like you're indoors. It doesn't look too fancy. You in guest lodgings?'

'We're not in the Adelaide Hills, but on a remote station in the mountains hundreds of miles from Adelaide. I'm nervous about it.' I waited for some comforting words, but she didn't seem like she'd heard me.

Her next line told me that she had indeed heard me. 'Well, just come home,' she said, tight-lipped. And there it was again: I had the strongest sense she lacked interest in anything I did in Australia. Then she was talking about herself, not having asked me one question – a familiar pattern.

When I finally asked her to repeat something because I wasn't following her, she said, 'I'm fed up.'

'About what?' I blew out air and looked at my nails. I was daring her to notice that I wasn't even feigning interest.

'It's these stupid legs. Do you ever get restless legs?'

I have spent a lifetime telling her I do not suffer from restless legs. I told her as calmly as I could, 'No, I don't have restless legs. Never have.'

She shook her head. 'You don't know how lucky you are. If I could lose this weight…but,' she shrugged, picking up an almost overflowing glass of white wine, 'I'll have to get back to the gym.'

'This will be the gym you've only ever had lunch in?'

We'd had this conversation too many times over the years, particularly since I've been in Australia. I had wanted to tell her about Amirda at night, and how scared I was. I wanted to share with her that I couldn't stop thinking was that someone looking at the house? We were lit up like a Christmas tree after nine p.m. I imagined once I'd said this to her, she would either agree with me or laugh at my silliness. I'd go on, People can see in but you cannot see out. When I looked through the black window of the sitting room, Mum, I was wondering if someone was looking in from the creek beyond or even was just right outside. We are so illuminated, it would be like watching a live TV show for the person outside. The light brings the bugs in too. It's bad enough having to watch your step to avoid geckos, lizards, mice and snakes. The light brings in moths and every kind of biting insect. Mum – you never know what's going to come running across the carpet. I'd wait for her to laugh. We did manage to find a lamp with a low-watt bulb, but now the place is virtually in darkness. It's like we can't win. Here, she might interrupt to offer some practical advice. Some hope. I never had conversations like this with her.

I heard Steve approaching. 'That's Steve, Ma, better go, lots to do.'

'Okay, 'bye, and get yourselves home!' She turned the off button before I could reply.

Her word 'yourselves' rang in my ears. She wanted me to return with Steve now? Well, she had never asked me how my marriage was going, not since Steve had surprised her with an upgrade ticket, which had to be compensation for his behaving badly that German holiday. Seems he had bought back her good opinion after all. She had told me Steve wasn't right for me, but minutes later he had sent her home business class and all was forgiven. She must have fallen in material love with him at that moment.

My mind went back to those foul-smelling sprouting potatoes in the cupboard. I remember trying to tell my mother about how horrible it had been to move potatoes exploding with rot, squirting putrid liquids into my face, all because Dad had put a bag of potatoes in the wrong place and forgotten about them. She had given me a cold stare that told me I was not to bother her with such distasteful stories. She even sneered which I took to mean that she thought I was laying on the martyrdom or something. I learned that what happened while she was 'away' did not interest her. Well, it didn't if the tale involved any indirect criticism. A harsh stance for a mother to take against her daughter in anyone's book, I imagine.

'You're looking lovely, Mrs,' said Steve.

His cheerfulness that morning made me smile. When Steve is in these moods, I could happily coast along, shelving my desire for flight. If we lived in a bubble where I didn't need friends or diversion or anything but his good humour, it might be possible.

## Gun Shots for Real

One of Steve's first major jobs was to nail down the sheets of metal on various outhouses and put back the ones that had blown off. He did so after one sheet narrowly missed him while he was filling up the ute with diesel. It came off the shed with the dead roo in it. Boy, did that poor animal stink when Steve dragged it out. After getting Cid's permission, Steve pulled down a couple of sheds altogether because they were beyond repair. We spent one day moving piles of corrugated metal around, which ended up in the junk graveyard, and that itself would have to be put into some sort of order. I made sure Steve weighted everything down, and even then, the visions of being decapitated by flying sheet metal never completely left me. I'd get jittery when the wind blew gale-force, which some days was non-stop. The winds whipped up anything not held down. It was like something out of the movie Twister. Some days, it really wouldn't have surprised me to see a cow flying overhead with a van full of storm chasers in pursuit of it led by Helen Hunt.

There were other urgent jobs too, like clearing leaves from the garden so that we could avoid snakes. Steve was also laying mouse traps, stuffing holes with wire wool, and oh, all the things you do to make a house less like a chicken shed. I set to work on clearing the office. It is where I was going to flesh out my psychological thriller – if the vital chores did one day cease.

That day did come sooner than expected. Steve was out fixing another burst pipe, but the house was clean and tidy (as much as it could be), the chickens were fed and watered, as were the sheep, and I was free to do as I pleased. I placed my laptop in front of a spider-free office chair and sat down to write. I lifted the lid on the laptop and opened the folder 'Locked in One Nest'. I read the notes on my 'story so far'.

Dr Alia Sullivan and Dr Mark Dunn are 'happily' married English lecturers and all seems well until, one evening while her husband is away, Alia finds a key to his locked study, and goes in only to find that he's researching how to kill a person using untraceable poisons on an ACER laptop she's never seen. She is perturbed to read that one of his studies is on how botulism is a toxin strong enough to kill a weak person. It forms in raw garlic and olive oil. Alarm bells ring when she thinks of how her husband's meal that he served her the night before was saturated in garlic olive oil that he did not put on his own dish.

When I looked out the window, my novel emptied out of my head. Feelings of being completely alone overwhelmed me. I closed the laptop – it was as though someone was doing it for me. I couldn't shake the feeling that someone must be secretly looking at me. There were so many doors around the property, and some didn't have a lock. Surely someone was opening one of the back doors right then.

I got up – I'd take a look around, maybe grab the spade. No, that was too paranoid. I would see that there was no one around. Yet creepy scenes from horror and suspense movies were tormenting me. It probably didn't help that I wasn't sleeping very well. I'd wake at every sound and lie there thinking, There is someone in the house this time. I could not look at the bedroom door without seeing a long rifle pushing it open. I was sure that the next time I woke up, I'd be staring down the barrel of one of Cid's Stoegers.

Then, would you believe, my fears became a reality. We were just on our way to bed when gunfire sounded – clear as a bell. Steve, all credit to him, told me to stay where I was and ran through the house, out onto the veranda. I was frozen to the spot as I counted ten more gunshots. They were in the distance, so I went to find Steve. The shots were ringing out from Bedlam paddock (I had good reasons for choosing Bedlam as its name).

'Phone Cid,' I said. 'Phone him now.'

'It will be the roo shooters, from Urdlu. Nothing to worry about. They're supposed to tell us when they're shooting but maybe they told Cid and he forgot to mention it.'

'But it's pitch dark. Why are they shooting at night?'

'I'll send Cid a text,' said Steve, huffing.

Cid rang minutes later and said he'd sent a message to the Aboriginal lady at Urdlu named Sherrie – she was the elder in charge of the small Urdlu community. She was known to many as Aunty Sherrie, but her and Cid had known each other from kids and they were on first-name terms. Cid rang again and said Sherrie would sort it all out. I was not happy with this vagueness. It sounded like no one knew what was going on.

I asked Steve, 'What if those roo shooters aren't from Urdlu? Who's really out there?' I had visions of rednecks, drunk on beer and whisky, riding wild across the paddocks looking for a townie couple to torture for fun.

Steve just said, 'It's the Urdlu boys. Stop worrying. Let's go to bed.'

My legs would hardly take me there. We were going to be murdered. However, when I looked at Steve's unconcerned face, I knew deep down that my head wasn't right.

## Who's Worse, My Mother or the Creepy Campers?

The shots had indeed come from licensed roo shooters at Urdlu. Aunty Sherrie had sent apologies and said we would be informed next time 'the boys' were going shooting in one of the paddocks. This was good news and went some way to calming my over-wrought nerves as did the daily chores. I came to almost want housework because it served as a deflection. When I got lost in scrubbing, sweeping or dusting, I wasn't looking out of the window imagining unwanted visitors.

Another job that was excellent in alleviating my mental jitters was the task of sorting out a field of age-old scrap metal that had been a dumping ground for decades, and was now a vast mangled tip behind the house. Our job was to move the lot and create separate identifiable piles of copper wire, iron, pickets, sheet metal, gates – the categories never ended. The trials of this epic task I won't bore you with, save to say that on those mornings of sorting, I was more concerned with avoiding snakes than snipers. In some ways, I should have felt like the poor miller's daughter in the Brothers Grimm tale. She has the impossible task of having to spin straw into gold because her stupid father boasted to the king that she had the powers to do so. The twist here was that I didn't want Rumpelstiltskin to come and sort out the mess of metal for me. I was happy to fill trailer after trailer no matter how much I sweated. Steve was impressed – for once.

Of course, the silly fears had not gone away, and one morning, after the manual labours, when I had tried to sit down to write, but couldn't because I thought I heard a back door slam, my mum rang. As I watched her pixelated face come into focus, I got excited that she might want to really talk for a change. A proper conversation was overdue.

She said, 'What's wrong?'

(I was still panicking over the mystery door slam). It was a relief. She cared, she wanted to know if I was okay – wow, it mattered to me that much.

'I know it's childish to be afraid, but I feel afraid when I'm alone and Steve just doesn't seem to care.'

She shook her head and said, 'That was your father all over. He always made a joke of anything I was serious about and used it as an excuse to go to the pub.'

To my amazement, she continued talking about how she wasn't taken seriously in her marriage – it was stuff I had never even heard, like she was making it up as she went along. The more she said 'your dad', the more I was getting agitated and my own thoughts took over.

My dad, my dad, the man who drank himself to death because he never got his shit together after you went 'away'. I had to run the home from hell and you never asked me one damn question about how I was coping. I was sixteen and had to manage the chaos on my own for six long months. Had to clear up evil messes like those sprouting potatoes that turned a kitchen cupboard into a fetid forest of evil-smelling freakishness. I had to live with three men who didn't know how to wash a shitting dish or pick up their underpants. But you never asked how I was coping, this was simply your time to be away. The tacit agreement was, still is, that you had no choice but to leave for six months, but you chose to leave all right.

'Is he there?'

I stared at my mother, then realised she was asking if Steve was with me. I told her he was up at the shed.

She said, 'You and Steve need to get home here and stop messing around in bloody "outback" Australia …'

'I'm not ten years old, Mum.'

'No, but you act it sometimes.'

I looked blankly at her as she was munching on a cake she shouldn't be eating, not least because it was late, but because she has diabetes. No point criticising. My mother doesn't 'do' criticism of herself. She has always been good at criticism of me, though. Example: the moment I phoned her with the news that I'd been awarded a PhD, and said the words 'I'm a doctor!' for the first time, her immediate response was, 'Dr Dolittle!' Hahaha. The worst of it was that the title stuck, and she amused friends and relatives with her bon mot. She wasn't interested that in my PhD research I had discovered the extent to which the Victorian novelist George Gissing had influenced Orwell, and the ways in which I demonstrated how Orwell developed innovative narrative techniques, thanks to Gissing, on free indirect thought. She was not curious about Charlie Chaplin's influence on Orwell's work that I found. Noooo, she couldn't give a flying f**k that Orwell learned much about comedy from Chaplin and 'borrowed' many of his techniques of bathos to get a laugh in Animal Farm and Nineteen Eighty-Four. Did she care about that? No, she cared more about getting a cheap laugh by calling me Dr Dolittle. Admittedly, when you read books while lying on a couch, it can give that impression – and I did read a lot.

'Look, Mum,' I said, interrupting who knew what part of her fantastic tale of woe, 'there's people coming, I'll have to go. Call you in a few days.'

'Oh, okay. I love you.'

I switched off the phone. Her 'I love you' didn't make me homesick, it just made me sick. Steve says, 'I love you' and 'I do love you, you know,' a lot, just like my mother. Love in my experience is something shown to you and not said. One of the oldest clichés is actions speak louder than words. That is a cliché for a reason.

It was true that people were coming, but not at that precise moment. Cid's campers had confirmed and were expected. I was determined not to fret unnecessarily and I was also set on getting some writing done on my psychological thriller.

I lifted the lid of my laptop and opened the Locked in One Nest folder. I read my notes.

> Alia wants to believe that she has a good marriage. When she discovers that her sickness and the metallic tasting food have a perfectly explainable cause (she's pregnant), and that the research

into poisons was not Mark's but simply what was left on an old computer Mark is fixing up for a student, she returns to her conviction that she loves her husband and he loves her and tells herself she was morbid, exhausted and had a hormonal imbalance, and that's why she could falsely entertain the idea that 'loving Mark' could be plotting to poison her.

Good. I had a lot to write about. I got stuck in. I wouldn't overthink – just write. Some hours later, I looked at the clock. Good. It was almost one and I hadn't even looked over my shoulder for an intruder! I would have some lunch and wait for the campers. Please let them be harmless, please let them be harmless.

The campers arrived. They were a couple of grey nomads in a big four-wheel drive pulling a caravan. They said they didn't need electricity because they were self-sufficient. I pointed to a spot in the creek where Steve had told me was a good spot for the nature campers.

'How long are you staying?' I asked.

They looked at each other, and he said, 'A week. We'll stay the week.'

I walked back to the house feeling rather proud of myself. I wasn't afraid. Result. I got a shock when half an hour later I went to see where they had set up camp only to find they were next to the house by the chicken shed. She waved and started to come over to talk to me. Her husband was looking on. I started getting creeped out. Now they wanted to be friends? Why weren't they in the creek? Why so close to the house? Was this the infamous Fred and Rosemary West who befriended people only to lure them to their death and bury them under their floorboards? Was she going to hold a shotgun to our heads while he sexually interfered with me? This was summer in the outback – what sane people, especially old people, travelled to isolated hot places full of snakes and no people? Wasn't it only crazies on the run from the Feds who wouldn't hesitate to shoot you in the guts and steel your credit cards after torturing you for the pin number – there are plenty of examples. I had to stop watching CSI.

However, she wasn't coming over for a chat or to get my pin number. She stooped to pick up something, looked like an item of clothing. It was then I saw they had a little washing line rigged up full of smalls. She started walking back to her husband.

I took a deep breath and swallowed a fly, perhaps two. I doubled up and tried to cough them out but only managed to make myself hot in the face. I closed my eyes, panting and hating myself, hating them, hating just about everything – was it hate?

When Steve came back, he looked exhausted. I felt a little guilty since I hadn't done much except sit in front of a closed laptop for most of the afternoon. I had wanted to get back to writing but couldn't. Maybe I was Dr Dolittle.

'Bad day out there, honey?' I asked, hoping to inject some genuine feeling of compassion into my voice. I was in a strange kind of mood, like I didn't know how or what to feel. I even wanted him to sit down next to me and say something nice, which probably would have made me clingy, and then I'd have taken it to the bedroom.

'Ah, I can't get a tank to stop overflowing,' he said, kicking his boots off, 'but I can't see what's wrong with the float. I've tried a new washer but…' He went on in detail about his trials.

When he finished, I told him the campers had arrived and I started to say, 'You won't believe what I've been thinking,' when he got up and said, 'I'll wander over and say g'day.'

Then he looked at me, looked at the laptop, and said, 'Have you done some writing today?'

'Heaps,' I lied. Well, I had done some in the morning, but that wasn't heaps.

'That's good,' he said, patting my shoulder, 'really good. When I get back, we'll have a beer, and you can tell me what you wrote about.'

I reminded him that we only had a few left as I watched him leave. I didn't worry about him reading my novel. He had stopped reading anything I wrote years ago. Plus, the less he knew, the more he would be himself and provide the psychological noir for my domestic thriller.

When he got back, he'd forgotten about my book and was all about how he didn't get to see the campers because they'd gone for a walk. They were way down the creek. We had a couple of beers, tea, then bed.

The next morning, I pulled back the bedroom curtain and saw the campers were sitting in deckchairs looking at the house. At us?

'What are you doing?' asked Steve. 'What's out there?'

I didn't dare share my idiotic fears about our guest campers being serial killers. Dealing with his heartless teasing might turn me killer.

# Please Don't Take Me to Mount Remote

There were more fears for me to overcome in my journey to the farthest regions of the station. A place that made my heart race was Mount Remote. Not wanting to stay with the creepy campers, I went with Steve on the water run. This time, the run included going out to the most westerly part where the station meets the desert. Beyond was a desolate place where many early pastoralists had met their demise while trying to find fertile land for their flock or cattle. For El Cid, here was pasture for goats. White goats too, with long beards, that looked like the stuff of ancient sacrifices. The goats were the only good thing about Remote. I knew if the goats were there, then no person was, because goats don't hang around when humans show up – they clear off up into the highest hills.

Mount Remote is a giant mountain like the Matterhorn. Cid told us that cameleers were often camping behind the mountain where it becomes desert, at least for parts of the year when they conducted tourism walking treks with the camels. I can't stand camels – they are dusty beasts frothing at the mouth and sneezing with bot fly – but I would have rejoiced if they had turned up at Mount Remote to take the edge off the tumbleweed feel. The bore at Remote was pumped with a Southern Cross windmill that creaked. Once the goats disappeared, the place was eerily still save for the mournful tune the windmill sail made. The whole place seemed to have an atmosphere – if there were unhappy spirits of past Aboriginals, I would believe it was here.

There was an old shepherd's or drover's hut made of stone at the base of the mountain. The roof had long gone. It was just two rooms, one with a fireplace. It was over a hundred years old. When I saw the cottage, my heart sank. It looked like a place for a fugitive to hide out. Here was water, shelter and isolation. When we inspected the house, there was evidence of a fire. Someone had been staying there.

It didn't help that when Steve phoned El Cid to tell him about the fire pit in the cottage, he said, 'Poachers. If you see those bastards, tell them to get off my land.' Oh, the rifle was already pointing right at us, I knew it.

As soon as we had cleaned the trough, I wanted to leave, but there was an underground leak indicating a pipe had burst. We'd have to stick around to sort it out. As Steve was turning off taps, I looked about for the poachers. This time it wasn't my fevered imagination, it was real. Poachers meant the men were outlaws. Steve got a spade from the ute and started digging. I looked at the car radio – there was no one in range from here. If I tried to send a mayday signal, chances are it would only signal to a fellow poacher that I was raising the alarm on their partner in crime.

An hour later, I was still jumpy. The mountains surrounding us were intimidating. There were huge square boulders at the base, some near my feet where they had tumbled down, great blocks of granite that would kill you if you got in their path. Many seemed precariously balanced at the top, ready to tip. Was it thousands of years or hundreds of years or a matter of minutes till a drop happened? Again, I had a feeling that the spirits of fallen Aboriginals could be along the top of that mountain, and might push a boulder down onto us new invaders. I don't know, it was a place where you felt someone could commit murder. There were plenty of recorded incidents of murders that had taken place in drovers' cottages like the one at Mount Remote – usually connected with cattle rustling or suspected theft of some sort. The Flinders Ranges has a turbulent history.

Lake Torrens was not that far away. It had not seen fresh water for some 35,000 years and was now not much more than salt-encrusted mud. The Aboriginals had named the lake Ngarndamukia, meaning 'shower of rain'. Its current name Torrens was due to some English guy, 'one of the founders of the colony of South Australia', according to the Wiki page I was able to access thanks to the Telstra tower nearby. Welcome to the modern age! Funny how almost every place, mountain or body of water in Australia is named after some guy, usually English or Scottish, who claimed to have 'discovered' it. The Aboriginal peoples, diverse as they were, had no such arrogance and covetousness to make individual claims on the natural world.

When Steve had got the pipe free and found the source of the leak, I fetched a saw, a mallet and wrenches as he got the stoppers that would plug the rest of the pipe back together when the holey bit was removed. I was happy when we were finally driving out, but wouldn't be completely so until we were well past the second gate. You had to cut through another station to get to Mount Remote, which meant lots of gate opening and closing. I hated being the one to get out of the vehicle to do that.

After tea that night, our usual feast of succulent chops, Steve's hasselback potatoes and signature roasted veg (he was becoming quite the gourmet), I wanted booze to settle my frayed nerves – okay, any excuse. Cid had mentioned there might be a case of wine from his vineyard in the cellar. As for the cellar, it took a while for Steve and me to summon up the courage to sweep away the leaves and spider sacs and put a new light in the little passage to the underground cellar, but we got there. Thankfully, the campers couldn't see us so they weren't likely to come over to say hello, or beat us to death on the stairwell and steal the booze for themselves.

The cellar was full of dusty bottles. We might be in luck. I pulled out one bottle from a shelf. The cork was mouldy. I put it back and pulled out another – the colour of the wine looked odd, too pale for red. Steve found a case of beer. It wasn't too dusty, which meant it was young. It looked like pure gold. Then we hit the jackpot – a case of Shiraz. A whole case of the stuff. I was about to take a holiday from my paranoia.

With nervous anticipation, we opened the first bottle of wine. It was divine. We sat at the kitchen table for hours and drank two bottles, plus some whisky that Steve hadn't told me about. I didn't care when the darkness descended. Let anyone look through the windows. I walked to the loo without putting the light on and slept without a care for the campers – they could have me if they wanted me. As for thieves, snakes, poachers, spiders, I didn't give a flying…

When I woke up at four a.m. wanting the toilet, I didn't get up, but waited until sunrise to make sure the coast was clear.

## Irrational Worries or Legitimate Fears?

With a woozy head, I watched the campers walking around outside – were they snooping? I had let Steve go pipe-checking on this own. I was nursing a hangover. I got to thinking about house break-ins in general; there seemed to be an epidemic of them in Australia – not in the outback, no, but the suburbs. There were public meetings about them in Queensland just then because too many break-ins ended in fatalities, hence the urgency for action. Maybe that's why grey nomads were taking to the road: 'Try and rob me now, ya bastards.' The day we picked up our campervan from the dealer, we had to wait while the owner finished talking to the police. Three of his second-hand cars had been stolen that night. He didn't seem devastated or even too surprised. Burglaries were rife in the area. Actually, it could have been the fact that he'd just ripped us off to the tune of thirty grand that he was not too down. God, the Bus was a thirty-grand piece of junk, now collapsed under a carport that might well be its final resting place.

As far as Amirda went, I needed to work out what was a silly worry and what was a legitimate fear. I laughed at myself for foolish ideas about stranger-danger, but I couldn't escape the cold fact that the place was wide open for the taking. The sheds had no locks and yet there were all sorts of treasures, from an armoury of guns to cabinets full of brand-new power tools and shiny designer spanners, wrenches, screwdrivers, all of it. The gun safe was indeed a safe, a safe with a dial lock, but it could still be picked up and carried away or crowbarred open. Wait – there were chainsaws in the garage. Couldn't the burglars just take one of those to the cabinet and cut a hole in it? They could.

As for the rest of the booty, each vehicle around the property cost tens of thousands of pounds and all of them had their keys left in.

Motorbikes galore, Cid had, big razzy 600 cc jobbies with keys in the ignition. The tractor alone was worth over a hundred grand, and there it was, ready to go, just like the CAT digger next to it with its state-of-the-art caterpillar wheels. The guy who sold us the Bus would say, 'That Cid is taking a bit of a risk.' I know he would.

There was so much more too: rows of brand-new tyres for the taking. There was even a bloody gas station on the grounds that wasn't locked up. I imagined other properties would be protected by dogs or just having lots of people around, or they'd have cameras. This place had nothing. There were no cameras, no guard dogs, no security, no nothing, just trust that no thieves would come your way, which was astonishing, given that complete strangers come and camp in the grounds and go on walkabout where they can see all this for themselves. Yes, the place hadn't been raided ever in its hundred-plus years of existence, so Cid had told us, but wasn't a raid overdue? Why didn't he have cameras that would alert you to someone crossing a gate or approaching the house?

Now I was thinking that the campers could be more like Bonnie and Clyde. They weren't sexual perverts, they'd just come to loot Amirda, or case the joint for someone else.

Was this a legitimate fear? A voice said it was not, but I couldn't judge for myself. By lunchtime, the aspirin and water had cleared my head so I sat down and opened Locked in One Nest. I got as far as this:

> Alia knows in her gut that the very fact of her thinking Mark capable of plotting murder must have its roots. Indeed, Alia's subconscious is constantly reaching out to have her 'wake up' to the warning signals Mark puts out: he is too secretive; he's too close to one of his female students; Alia's word has no sway with him, yet he is ruled by his father. Mark tells lies about where he goes and what he spends. When Alia gets a book deal, Mark can barely congratulate her. There is also the mystery of why an academic snob like Mark is compromising his personal and professional integrity by promoting a student who is a semi-literate plagiarist.

I tried to flesh out the story and build the dialogue, but everything I wrote I erased. Did I have writer's block? Or perhaps it was Ali's book deal that was playing on my mind. I couldn't get out of my head what had happened to me when I got my academic tome published. Ashgate offered me a book deal while I was a lecturer, but at a laughable 2.5% royalty for me. I got a few thousand pounds in the wake of the publishing of The Unsung Artistry of George Orwell, but to think what it could have been if they had done any real marketing to universities and schools like they promised, and if the book had been affordable (it was over £100), and if I had got a decent percentage. I thought, I will get Alia a much higher percentage and her book will be a global success, not a damp little squib that academia ignores because I didn't go to Oxbridge and have no connections. Bitter? You bet.

A few days of sitting and doing little at my laptop passed. It wasn't surprising that I was liking wine more and more in the evening. A few beers and a glass or two of wine chased away the demons in my head. It's a funny thing, alcohol. It can transform you from a paranoid mess to someone who's happy to enter a dark cellar with only a weak torchlight to save you. I know, because it happened to me, was happening to me. Yes, I know, it's a dangerous opiate for those with a troubled mind, and so I knew I would have to stop.

In any case, the wine-induced serenity was fleeting, and now my HRT (hormone replacement therapy, in case you don't know) was running out. I'd got my mum to send patches out, but finally, when I failed to show in person at the surgery back home, they cut off the supply. I had been on HRT since my hysterectomy, which I had because my uterus was full of cysts. I only discovered I was funny-shaped when I went on a three-month exercise and detox regime. I was tired of looking like a potato, but when I lost the weight, I looked pregnant. The GP thought I was pregnant. The upshot was, the cysts had to come out. I didn't want children, so a full hysterectomy wasn't a problem for me.

I had been trying to make the patches last longer, because the clinic at Leigh Creek was a mystery to me. I knew it opened seldom, or that was my belief. However, the night sweats were coming back, and I wanted to kill Steve more than usual. I wondered whether my brain fog might also be responsible for the writer's block.

About day four into the campers' stay, I was staring at my laptop when I heard the chickens squawking. They kept it up for over ten minutes and I knew that if I didn't go to investigate, I was a snivelling coward. There could be a snake in the coup or a kangaroo, or any manner of things. What I feared most was that the campers were in there, but I was too scared to prove myself wrong in case they really had set up an ambush to lure me out, whereupon they'd tie me up and do heaven knew what with me. If you think I'm joking, I'm not!

Finally, I banged my fists on the table and got up. It was a relief not to have to stare at my laptop any more. Maybe a painful death at the hands of deviants was what I deserved for failing to take any positive action in my life. I put some boots on and went to investigate what was making the chickens flap about in high dudgeon. Collecting the eggs was also overdue. I braced myself, but by the time I got to the hens, whatever was bothering them had stopped. Hens do have a pecking order, so perhaps one of the lower orders was trying to have more than its share of water or had hogged a shady spot reserved for the chief squawker. I got the eggs and tried to sneak away without being seen by the campers, who I had spied by their tent. But the woman saw me. She waved at me, and I waved back, then she started pointing in the distance. I walked through to the orchard, going closer to the fence. She was pointing at a family of emus! I went to shout, but she put a finger to her mouth. Of course, yes, I shouldn't scare them away. There was mum and dad emu and a row of chicks following behind. I quietly made for the gate so I could go down and have a look at the emu chicks. On the way, I passed the campers' little makeshift clothesline. This time they'd put out other clothes to dry…maybe they were normal after all. The emu family had not noticed us and were crossing the creek at a leisurely pace.

When I got to her, she whispered, 'Isn't it a wonderful sight. You are so lucky to live here.'

I smiled.

She said, 'Would you have a bit of cake with us?'

'That would nice,' I said, and we walked up to their caravan.

What can I say? All was perfectly normal, of course. They started telling me about how much they were enjoying themselves. They had met in India when they were young backpackers and volunteer workers at a school for orphans. The heat of Amirda was making them nostalgic… I listened to them for over an hour, and we chatted about all sorts. They were interested in how I came to be there and how I was coping with the isolation and so on.

When I left them, hot tears of shame stung my eyes. I had to run to the house, but broke down before I was even through the door. Great sobs wrenched me. It was misery, knowing I was ludicrous, but I couldn't cure myself of it.

Then, I had another thought, a kind of a comic epiphany – maybe I just needed my hormone replacement patches! I dried my tears and for the first time at Amirda, I felt there might just be some hope for me. Although, I knew – oh I knew – that if I had any real shot at inner peace, personal fulfilment, call it what you will, I needed that three-dimensional magic-eye picture of my psyche (or is it soul) to reveal itself to me. Do you know those images? There was a whole book of them, brought out in the 90s. The picture appears to be some random pattern that looks like a piece of modern artwork. But if you squint at it and concentrate, before long a clear and vivid scene is revealed. I felt that if I only knew how to look at my mind in the right way, I might see some clear and vivid picture of what was making me restless and dissatisfied with life.

# What do Aussies Have Against Whole Words?

The Wests – they had a name now, not just the campers – had gone. I missed them – how about that? I walked down to where they had stayed and walked through the dirt where they had made their mark, literally. They were now history, but something positive had happened.

I still wasn't writing anything I could save. I acted satisfied in the bedroom instead of trying to talk to Steve about what was bothering me. Steve being nice wasn't helping with the noir side of my psychological thriller. When Steve is nice, I can't picture him dark. And making love to him kept him very nice indeed, not to mention not talking to him about my neurosis. I often wonder if I have some kind of Stockholm syndrome when it comes to this marriage. When he gets nasty or tells me, 'No', I can't invite so and so around, or whatever it is, I don't argue any more, but just vow I'll leave him and therefore it doesn't matter. He hasn't won, but then days later when he's all nice, I forget that I was mad at him and go back to liking him, but it's all because we're in this bubble and frankly, because he's getting his own way. Ergo, I am changing to suit him and thinking all is calm, all is well because I don't discuss anything that he can't understand, or refuses to understand. I'm probably a bit of a Stepford wife by now – you know, programmed to be submissive to her husband and be happy in the role. They made it into a movie. Everyone who meets us thinks we're the perfect couple because I'm always smiling and talkative and Steve's always shy but affable.

So ran my thoughts on the way to Leigh Creek to see the doctor to get some HRT. Unfortunately, we had to go there via Mount Remote to check that the pipe Steve had mended had not burst open again, it hadn't mended the first time. We were just about to hit the bitumen of the main highway when we passed a convoy of cars parked up on the side. There were over twenty cars, all parked in a row. In the distance you could see a movie scene was in motion – the long fluffy microphone on a stick was the giveaway. Actors were in town. Cid had told us we might see this sort of thing. He got a cut from the producers because they filmed on Amirda property.

'Why so many cars?' I said, more to myself than to Steve, but he had the answer.

'El Cid said actors won't travel together, they have to be alone.'

We'd see a lot of such film-crew convoys up and down the Flinders Way, and it did seem like the actors had to travel separately – I presume it has to do with learning lines, but I really don't know.

Thinking of why the actors travelled alone and forced so many vehicles on the roads was a nice distraction while we were on our way to Mount Remote. I didn't think of poachers until we got to the first gate, which was open! I felt sick. This wasn't right. The gate even had a placard on it saying 'Shut the Gate Mate'.

'There's bike tracks, look,' said Steve.

'How many?' I asked, looking all around to see if I could spot a biker.

'Ah, just one bike by the looks,' said Steve massaging his chin.

Steve got back in the ute and I closed the gate after us, dying to ask him if we could not bother about going to Mount Remote, but that would have been pointless.

When we got to the second gate, that too was wide open and there was a fresh bike track running ahead of us. I was thinking poacher. I didn't want to look any more in case I saw a wild man with a rifle slung over his shoulder riding around with a manic grin on his face. Having no respect for the country rules was a criminal trait. Do you know that it's usually criminals who park in disabled spaces because they have no respect for law or other people? That's a fact. I was thinking of all sorts of antisocial behaviour and getting really spooked.

I said, 'This could be trouble, couldn't it?' and hoped Steve would laugh at my overreaction. I needed to hear that I was getting this all wrong.

His reply was, 'Yep, it could be.'

'Then we shouldn't go to the trough.'

He looked at me and frowned. 'We're not turning back – if there is someone there, they need to leave.'

I covered my face with my hand and turned away. Why did we have to do this today? I moaned internally with frustration. If there was drama, I could miss my appointment with the doctor. And I needed my HRT. I opened my eyes to see Steve staring at me. He nodded at the gate. Oh, he was waiting for me to shut it. We were in another farmer's paddock.

When I rejoined Steve in the car, I breathed out and told myself to be calm. It was probably just a kid razzing around on his bike. As we drove, I noticed there weren't any goats. This biker had no doubt scared them away. When we got to the well, I looked around before getting out of the car. I couldn't see anything. Steve got out and went to inspect the pipeline. The ground was dry, and the water was flowing, so there were no issues.

'Let's go then,' I shouted out of the window.

'Trough needs another clean. The goats have crapped in it big time,' said Steve, pulling a brush out of the back. 'You giving me a hand?'

Bloody goats – they really do crap in their own water. As I got out, I saw something behind some trees. There was movement.

'Steve, there's someone there,' I whispered, pointing.

He looked. 'Where?' he said, his face clouding over.

I indicated as best I could the shadowy figure behind a large fallen gum tree. There was no doubt. There was someone hiding. A clear noise like coughing came from that direction.

'Who's there?' shouted Steve.

My insides flipped and my knees literally went weak. I edged towards the door of the ute. I'd jump in and drive at the guy if he had a gun. Steve started walking down to where the figure was hiding. I watched him, my eyes like saucers.

When Steve reached the tree trunk, there was a great rattling sound.

'Hey, calm down,' said Steve, peering into the foliage.

I had to admit he was brave. Then he disappeared.

'Shall I bring the car?' I shouted.

'No, just get me the wire cutters will you? It's a big red with its feet tangled in wire.'

I breathed out. I didn't even realise that I'd been holding my breath.

The poor kangaroo had got caught up in a roll of discarded fencing. Both its feet were wrapped up tight in the wire – it was horrible to look at, and he was twisting around, making more loops around his long feet. I handed Steve the cutters.

The roo tried to box Steve when he went near it. At times, Steve looked like he was fencing with a sword. I imagined him saying 'en garde' as he lunged forward to make a snip, then pulled back quickly before the kangaroo could land him an uppercut.

Steve decided to change tack and snipped at other parts of the wire, but the upshot was that the roo bounded off with his feet entwined in wire. It was awful to see him disappear over a hill with that wire on his feet. I suppose fences are to kangaroos and emus what ocean netting is to sharks and dolphins.

With frayed nerves, once again, I got to the medical centre. I was half an hour late. Steve went to do our grocery shopping as I sat down among the other patients and thought, You have no idea what I've just been through. Then again, this was the outback – perhaps trapped roos were common.

The flown-in doctor came out in person. I sensed he was English.

When my turn came to go in, I said, 'Your accent sounds familiar. Are you English?'

'From Manchester,' he said, peering at his computer screen, I guessed looking at my details the receptionist must have just keyed in.

I said, 'Manchester, that's what Aussies call bed linen here.'

'It is,' he laughed.

I said something about if the cotton mills of industrial England had been in Liverpool or Bristol, that's what the bedding section in the department stores would be called here. I was happy to carry on with this idea, but he said abruptly, 'How can I help you?'

'I need some HRT patches.' I got out an old HRT box so he could see what kind I wanted. I wondered whether to tell him that if I didn't get this dose of oestrogen either Steve's life or mine was probably in danger. I was expecting him to say that I looked too young to be on HRT and I was ready with my 'I had to have a full hysterectomy when I was –'

'Let's take your blood pressure then,' was all he said.

It took several goes for it to come down, because I suffer from 'white-coat syndrome'. I was dreading him telling me that I couldn't have the prescription because my blood pressure was too high, and I was getting ready to beg, but he said, 'If you'll wait in the surgery, should be about ten minutes.'

I was done. But before I left, he said to me, 'It's important that you check your blood pressure regularly because it can change, and if it's high then you really shouldn't be taking HRT. You could be at risk of blood clots. I suggest you get a heart monitor. They come with apps for your smartphone these days. They're very good.'

'Thanks, doctor, I will,' I said with no intention whatsoever of getting my own blood pressure pump. It's whitecoat syndrome, that's all it is – they told me so when I had the hysterectomy.

I had to wait my turn to see the receptionist, because there was a glut of people booking themselves in, or booking a relative in; there was a confusion of family members. I sat down until the chaos stopped. When the coast was clear, I went up and asked for my HRT.

The receptionist, who was different to the woman who initially signed me in, said, 'Do you have a script?'

'A script?' I repeated, thinking I must have misheard.

She nodded. 'Yes, do you have your script?' Then she smiled.

Script – an acting reference? The actors were probably staying at Leigh Creek Tavern – the only accommodation for miles. Was she joking with me, thinking I was one of the actors staying here, perhaps one of them was getting some medication? Or was lack of HRT and worry over that roo making me a little crazy?

I said, 'I'm not one of the actors.' Then I laughed, hoping she'd explain herself.

Her smiled vanished and she frowned. She said what came across as a very rude 'Sorry?'

I said, feeling my stress levels soar, 'No, I'm sorry, I don't understand what you mean. Why would I have a script?'

She frowned more and shook her head. She said, 'It's a simple question. Do you have your script?'

I barked. 'Script? Are you joking with me? Why would I have a script?' It took everything I had not to add, 'for fuckssake'.

Laughter erupted all over the packed waiting room.

Someone said, 'She don't know you mean prescription.'

It was the receptionist's turn to collapse with laughter. Prescription, of course. I forgot the doctor had given me one, probably because of the commotion before and my having to wait so long. I took the prescription from my pocket and handed it over. I had to take a seat again while she got it ready. People began to talk to me about how funny it was that I thought she was taking about actors. I was so embarrassed, I wished they'd shut up.

And there was more of this farce to come. After I had received my packets of HRT and paid for the prescription, the receptionist said, 'And it's sixty dollars for your console too.'

'My console?' I queried, dreading that I didn't understand yet again. Then, ha-ha! The penny dropped. The doctor had said I had to monitor my blood pressure. He'd gone and bloody ordered a blood-pressure monitor for me. Cheek, I thought, at sixty bucks.

I said, 'If that console is for monitoring blood pressure, I won't take it because I don't need to monitor myself at this stage.'

Again, there was that awful ripple of laughter around the surgery. The receptionist, laughing again, said, 'Your consult is your consultation with the doctor, that's sixty dollars.' Not 'console'!

I burst out, 'Jesus, script, consult, can you not use a whole word in this country?'

To this there were hoots of laughter, particularly from one Aboriginal woman who slapped her friend on the back and said, pointing at me, 'She's right!'

# A Local Speaks to Us!

With the ute door for privacy, I ripped open an HRT sachet and slapped the patch on my hip. Hopefully by the morning, I would resemble a sane human being again. We had decided to have lunch at the pub and, as we got out of the ute at Copley, I had a moment of – what to call it – happiness, a feeling of normality. It couldn't be the HRT working that quickly, could it?

Copley pub is an original Aussie saloon bar you could imagine Ned Kelly having a beer at. They have character, these places, with their walls covered in photographs spanning a hundred years, showing the first locals, and those over years, they show the old beer pumps and so on too. There are also painted portraits of bygone patrons. People go to these pubs for a yarn. While Steve was trying to read all the Copley cricket paraphernalia on its walls, from across the bar, I was gabbling to him about my 'script' and 'console' confusion. He shook his head as though I was a real ditz.

'Hey,' I said, about to complain of his lack of sympathy, but when I took an ice-cold beer from the landlord, I shrugged and said, 'I amused the locals, anyway.'

I was grateful that there weren't any of the people from the clinic in the pub, but I kept looking to check. I was safe. Almost everyone was in work gear. They would be from the water company or working in the mines perhaps, maybe road repairs. I got a nod of 'hi' from a couple of Aboriginal women in high-vis shirts, although their narrowed eyes stayed on us a little too long. Perhaps they were wondering which station we belonged to.

Then someone spoke to us, a bearded guy in a big blue farmer shirt. From under his big hat, he asked about Amirda and Cid because he recognised the ute. Steve swapped a few pleasantries with him until our lunch interrupted. I was startled by the size of the lunches. Each plate was covered with a giant schnittie, as they call them. It looked like the chef had butterflied a whole chicken and used a whole loaf to crumb it. Underneath was a plate full of hot chips (you can't just say 'chips', which are Pommie crisps). The meal could feed a family!

'That's a feast,' I said and felt like I was telling the whole bar, because everyone was staring at us.

I guess they wanted to hear Steve tell the bearded guy more about what we were doing at Amirda or more to the point, what Cid was doing these days, although there we couldn't enlighten people much.

Then beardy said something which shocked me. He said, 'You got terrorists staying at Amirda?'

Steve said, 'No.'

The guy went, 'Had some unwanted bikers on my property. Wondered if they was staying on Amirda. They need to be told not to drive around upsetting my cattle. But maybe they was from Kurra Weena. They got a lot of terrorists staying there.'

This was too much for me. I said, 'Why do you call them terrorists?' I was thinking they might have run amok out near Mount Remote.

Laughter erupted just like in the medical centre.

He said, 'I said tourists. You want to take the cotton wool out your ears, girlie.'

My face flushed scarlet and Steve shook his head slowly at me. In the end, I was able to laugh it off. At least we were getting to know people.

We didn't have another pint because we were too stuffed from the oversized schnitzel. There was a lot of conversation in the bar about the rains that were coming. Some said they didn't believe the drought would end; others were saying, 'There's gonna be a deluge like we haven't seen in ten years. I'm telling you, those creeks are going to run again.' I was selfishly hoping that any rain might hold off for another few months, because then Cid and his wife would close Amirda and I'd be back in Adelaide, where it was easier to get on a plane.

We went to the bottle-o in the next room before leaving, to get a case of beer and some wine. We also had to go back to the shops – Steve hadn't got half the stuff we needed because I had the shopping list.

The store at Leigh Creek wasn't like a remote store in England, or the people didn't act the same. Here, as a stranger, you were mostly ignored. Maybe it was because of the many people who passed through that the locals took little interest in a new face – or two new faces in our case. In small country towns in England, shopkeepers will be nosy with newcomers, downright invasive. For sure, you won't get your bottle of milk or loaf of bread until the person behind the counter has found out your business in the area.

Example: 'You passing through or just staying a while? You're staying? Where? How long for? You renting or did you buy? Just the two or you, or do you have children? Who you working for? Pays well? Oh, you work for yourselves, doing what exactly?' And so on and so forth.

In this isolated outback town, you would have no fears about protecting your privacy. You might as well have been invisible. Four people worked in the general store, and even when it was clear that we couldn't be just passing through, after say, our fourth visit, still not one person gave us a look of recognition or curiosity. I ceased to make polite chit chat. The crumpled face in reply to my 'Good to see you get fresh produce out here,' or similar, told me they continued to wear the T-shirt that said, 'Tell someone who gives a shit'.

That evening, Steve and I had a bit of a party. We danced, skitted the locals, made fun of the guy with the beard who said 'terrorists' instead of 'tourists', and all kinds of nonsense. This is what Steve and I do best. We get merry, we get silly, but we only do it when we are completely alone, and not that often, but when we do, I love it, I love him. This was how it was when we first got together. The map-maker and the teacher who worked hard and played hard and I daresay were the envy of many a lonely singleton or tepid couple. But gradually Steve changed when in company with other people. He got arsy, was prone to taking the hump by insisting my joke was at his expense. I grew nervous in a group situation lest I embarrass him. I hoped it would pass but it got worse, and I could feel that old tension when Cid was around. Was that emotional control – my nervousness triggered along the same principle as the hunger of a Pavlov dog? Or something else entirely?

## The Six-year Drought Was Coming to an End

A few weeks or so after I was regularly using HRT, I felt good, positive, and I was writing again – how the novel was flowing out of my fingers. This was where I was up to.

> The extent of Mark's lying is revealed to Alia when she returns to his locked study and finds fresh research on the ACER laptop into poisons and their ability to kill without leaving a trace. Alia also discovers a newspaper clipping in Mark's desk. It tells of a dentist who murdered both his wives by inducing a heart attack. Having them ingest lethal doses of calcium gluconate and potassium phosphate (substances that go undetected and give the appearance of a naturally suffered heart attack). Alia is horrified to see, on Mark's ACER laptop a search for how to source calcium gluconate and potassium phosphate. Now she is sure that Mark is planning her murder, or someone's murder. She believes she is safe FOR NOW because she is carrying his child. Alia observes how Mark is obsessed with becoming a father and emulating his head of department hero, Bill Lorenzo, who melts hearts with his 'out there' fatherhood. Indeed, the more Alia looks closely at her husband, the less and less she recognises the man she married.

I was bashing out some dialogue between Bill Lorenzo and Alia when Steve asked me, 'What's your novel about again?' He went to the kitchen and got some water.

I was stumped for a minute but I had a while to think because Steve was busying himself putting sauce bottles into neat lines in the cupboard – he was developing an eye for such pedantic detail in the kitchen and in our bathroom. It was his preoccupation with order that gave me the idea for Mark's obsessive-compulsive behaviour in the book, of course greatly exaggerated. And regarding the novel, I didn't want to tell him too much in case I inadvertently revealed something of my true feelings about our marriage, but then I thought better of it. He could do with a heads-up. After all, it wouldn't do for him to be totally blindsided when I came to announce THE END.

I said, 'It's a domestic noir, a psychological thriller about a woman who thinks her husband is trying to kill her.' Of course, Steve wasn't trying to kill me – I'll just clear that up.

'Hmm,' he said, pulling down his mouth. 'That sounds – heavy. Why did I think you were writing a romantic novel?'

I didn't remind him that he'd ceased taking an interest in my writing long ago. I was just glad that he was impressed enough by how I was glued to the chair that he left me alone.

Soon after Steve left, I was disturbed by the surprise arrival of El Cid. At least it was a surprise to me – Steve had forgotten to mention it.

El Cid was charmingly apologetic for interrupting my writing, but I packed up quickly and gave him a hand – he had come laden with goodies for us. He lugged his car fridge in. It was filled with lamb and beef from his own stock, which his butcher had transformed into all kinds of cuts, joints and sausages. We would continue to live like kings, and might perhaps develop gout if we weren't careful!

'Hope you like French muck too,' he said in his booming, jolly voice, putting a bag on the table. It was full of pretty jars.

I pulled one out and read, 'Paté de foie gras.' 'How come you have this if you don't eat it?' I asked.

'Guests leave it, probably because we give them wine.'

I thought of the guest accommodation at his Adelaide Hills property and felt a pang of envy that I wasn't there myself. I looked through the rest of the bag. There were pots of jam, truffle oils, different olive oils and olives, plus cheeses.

'It's like something you find in a picnic hamper from Fortnum & Mason,' I said.

'From who?' His face was all crinkled up.

I laughed and said, 'Never mind.'

He looked like he'd already forgotten.

He'd come up to make sure that Steve had cleared the gutters in preparation for the heavy rains that were due, that everyone was praying would come. The gutters fed rainwater into the many holding tanks around the homestead – most of them were getting dry and had been previously filled with trucked-in water.

I got the impression Cid spent his life driving along the Flinders Ranges Outback Highway and whatever highway takes you to Broken Hill. I didn't manage to earwig any of his conversations with his mistress, but I was hopeful of getting somewhere. For sure, it was still on with those two if his hushed conversations in mole-c\*\*t were anything to go by.

That evening I did 'tea' and cooked up one of his lamb joints. I liked to make a show of spoiling El Cid. It irked Steve that I did a full roast dinner every night, baked apple crumble with custard, and was happy to make a full English breakfast for us all every morning.

'He'd probably be happy with a bit of toast and cereal,' said Steve one morning as I sizzled sausages in the pan, grilled tomatoes, whipped up scrambled eggs and the microwave went 'ding' signalling the beans were ready.

'Please just watch the toast,' was my curt reply.

At the beginning, I enjoyed the novelty of playing 'mum' in the country kitchen while the men did the hard yakka outdoors. Steve was probably right to get a little fed up because I was a little hyperactive in the kitchen and got upset if things weren't right with the breakfast.

El Cid would say, 'No hurry, it's all good,' and Steve would look like he was having a private seizure as I jumped up to get the brown sauce I'd forgotten to put on the table.

Cid complimented me on how tidy the cupboards were these days and joked about not wanting to mess anything up, but it was Steve who was responsible for the neatness around the kitchen, the symmetry of the coffee and tea containers and so on. However, I knew better than to say it was down to Steve, who would have been mortified in case the farmer thought him a 'Mary-Anne', something like that. Steve's neatness comes from his army training; its roots lie in machoistic sergeant drills not femininity.

The hard yakka outside lasted from dawn to dusk and often beyond that when El Cid visited. This time was no exception. Work around the homestead was full on too. The rains were coming sooner than predicted and Cid needed Amirda to be prepared.

It seemed extraordinary that, while people were still putting out fires all over the state in blistering temperatures, a biblical deluge was on its way thanks to the La Niña weather system – or was it El Niño? The difference confuses the hell out of me – one does southern oscillations, the other the cha-cha-cha. Whatever, about the second week in February, dark clouds began to form above Amirda.

Cid had warned Steve to turn back if the rain started while we were out. 'Turns into a mudslide out there very fast,' were his words. It didn't matter if he hadn't turned off bores, or completed the water run. Getting back was a priority because if the ground got too wet, 'You might never make it back,' said El Cid without a trace of mirth – most unusual for him.

We had just finished cleaning Camel-foe when the sky got dark.

I looked up and said, 'Maybe we should go back now.'

Steve looked at the sky and got out his phone. 'There's rain coming but not till later. We can do up to the top of Rocs and come back.'

I protested, 'Rocs is all the way up to TC' (a neighbouring station).

He looked out again and gave me some north-easterly or east-northerly analytical claptrap about wind direction. We would be in front of any rain, he assured me. And you know what's coming, right?

From trough to trough, I was getting more and more nervous, because the clouds in the distance were getting blacker while you blinked. It was definitely raining hard in the distance, and covering a wide area. We did make it to Rocs but didn't get out of the ute. A bolt of lightning cut through the blackness in the near distance, then another bolt and another. Great cracks of thunder followed.

'I know a short cut back,' said Steve.

I didn't dare reply because I wanted to tell him he was a reckless idiot. And it turned out that there was no short cut. We were hours away, even if he took the diagonal route.

We started driving into rain. There was cracking thunder and bolts of lightning all around us. The ute started to slip and slide. Steve assured me that we'd be on firmer ground soon, but the wheels were spinning in the mud. He tried to make a turn, which made it worse, and it felt like all the tyres were whizzing around and we were going nowhere but down. Then sure enough, we were bogged and going nowhere.

'Fuckssake,' yelled Steve as he got out into the rain. He now had to put the front wheels into four-wheel drive setting.

I was chanting prayers that we'd make it back. Steve got back in soaking wet, his boots caked in mud – the ground had turned into soft-scoop chocolate ice cream. Or better say dog poop, because that's how nasty it made you feel. He put the car into four-wheel gear and managed to get us out of the bog. Only to get stuck again. The rain was now so heavy that the windscreen wipers couldn't clear it.

Now I was shouting, 'Cid told you to turn back if it –' I shut up. Steve's dark look was menacing and, yes, I wasn't helping.

With his mouth snarling and his teeth clenched, he said, not looking at me, 'What the fuck do you know about anything?'

I was scared, not only of getting bogged for the day, but of him. Steve revved the ute and I thought, if we don't move, he's going to lose his mind. We did move and Steve drove at top speed. At one point, I thought he might roll the car, his driving was that erratic, but soon the ute righted itself, Steve slowed down and we were driving in lighter rain on harder ground.

Neither of us said a word to each other all the way back. I don't remember ever being so grateful to get out of a car, which was a mess, like it had been coated in mounds of sticky clay. You couldn't see any of the chassis. I didn't offer to help clean the vehicle, leaving Steve to it. It was definitely his mess, though I did pretend like I wanted to help before getting the hell out of his way.

Half an hour later, the thunder and lightning was overhead and the homestead was getting drenched. Steve came over to me – I was sitting at the office table pretending to write – I was merely staring at words.

He gave me a kiss on my forehead and said, 'Sorry about that.'

I patted his hand on my shoulder. 'Well, I think the drought's over,' I said.

'The ground is so dry that this storm won't do much,' was his reply.

I shook my head a little. 'Whatever you say, dear,' I said, getting up. I often use 'dear' when I want to inject some criticism without upset. 'I'll put the kettle on,' I said, 'I need some coffee.'

At that moment, there was a deafening crack outside, then a sizzle. Then the fan stopped above us.

'The electricity's out. Lightening just hit that electricity pole,' said Steve.

Then the drama began. Steve had to pull the heavy generator out and hook it all up. We had to stop the deep freezers from melting, and the fridges. It was still hot and nothing would last long turned off. I couldn't believe how many cable bundles Steve brought over.

Soon the floors were strewn with cables, which looked like ropes ready for mountaineers to pick up and scale Everest. It was my job to collect up the cables and plug them in to various sockets. Soon I was balancing precariously on chairs trying to plug in at points that seemed to be in the most impossible of places, either too high, too low, or too concealed behind white goods to reach with any ease. I wondered if it was why Steve was losing his grip – everything around this place seemed set on winding you up. I groaned through my teeth as I made one last push to plug the Internet cable into a socket behind a ton-weight filing cabinet.

When everything was finally plugged and set to go, Steve fired up the generator. Nothing. It wouldn't splutter into life. After a few more futile turns of the key, Steve re-checked the fuel. There was none.

'How'd I miss that?' he said.

I didn't dare say, 'I wonder?'

Off he went to get a jerrycan of fuel.

While Steve poured petrol into the generator, he covered my feet several times because he tipped the jerrycan too much. I had to turn away from the choking fumes. Steve was copping his share too and coughed his guts up a few times. If someone had put a match to us, we would have been burned alive.

But we had success eventually, and the generator started. The noise wasn't great. A pair of industrial headphones wouldn't have gone amiss, but at least the freezer meats were saved.

The rain continued to pour and pour and pour. Soon we were looking at overflowing gutters.

'I should have cleaned out the gutters better,' said Steve while we were looking at water jets gushing from all corners of the house, depriving the water tanks of maximum rain deposits.

I put my head in my hand – why hadn't he cleared them properly? What had he been doing on the roof all that time? Cid would spew. Now the homestead looked like some bizarre theme-park water feature.

'Ah, the tanks will probably fill anyway,' he said with a frown.

I told myself to back off being critical. I really shouldn't be so harsh on him. He had a lot to manage on the station. It was no caretaker role really, and maybe being out there in blistering heat every day, and often alone, was causing his brain to get a little overcooked. Not one day passed without something needing fixing, and it was never straightforward. Often, he had to come back to get parts and go back out and he wouldn't even stop for a cuppa.

That night, gale-force winds raged through the trees and around the house, sounding like an invading army of angry monsters. Rain beat down heavily on the roof and objects flew and banged about.

'Jesus, the ceiling could fall in,' said Steve, as we lay in bed unable to sleep.

## Our Driveway Has Turned Into the Rapids

The rain battered the roof all night, although there were lulls, and soon we could hear frogs – hundreds or thousands of croaking frogs.

'They must hibernate in the creek bed,' I said.

Steve sat up.

'What is it?' I asked.

He said, 'The frogs coming back to life means the creek is flowing. It's been six years since the creeks flowed, apparently.'

We had to wait for morning to find out. Our morning started at seven, not five.

Sure enough, the creek was flowing. We watched the rushing brown water passing by the house. That was our way out, but not any more. We were now cut off from the outside world. I was liking this. The rain suddenly got even heavier. The clattering noise above sounded like a plane was dropping tons of cutlery on the house. No wonder, when the roof is made of corrugated iron. What is it with Australians and tin roofs?

The rain didn't let up all day, and Steve was having to empty the rain gauge so it could get filled up again. By about four o'clock, another sound added to the chaos raging outside. The creeks were flowing all around the house and the main one out front was now a raging torrent. We heard a rip.

'That's a tree falling,' said Steve.

We ran out onto the veranda. What a sight! Huge gums were careering across what was yesterday a driveway.

'I need my phone. I got to film this,' I said running back in.

Ten minutes later, Steve was pulling his shirt over his head, and then his shorts were off, undies too. He ran starkers onto the lawn and down to the creek. What the hell – there were no cameras to film us. Excitedly, I threw my clothes off and ran after Steve. Wearing only boots, we stood at the edge of the creek looking at the debris hurtling passed us. The rain gauge had measured sixty millimetres. Later there was another sixty, and just now, another eighty. Australia's long drought was over. Perhaps I might have been afraid that the house could flood but it was up too high for that – the foundations might be compromised but no water from the creeks had ever entered the house, Cid assured us.

'Wait here,' said Steve, running back to the house. In minutes, he was back with beers. 'We ain't going anywhere for a while. Might as well have a party and toast the rain Gods while we're about it.' He handed me a stubby.

Drinking beer against the rage of the waters, I started doing a silly dance, singing, 'A sailor went to sea sea sea, to see what he could see see see, but all that he could see see see, was the bottom of the deep blue sea sea sea.'

No one could reach us, no one could see us. I was liberated by the flowing waters all around.

I slept well too. I didn't think about roofs falling in. I knew that we couldn't be reached by anyone on foot and certainly not by car, nor even by boat – the flowing waters were too gnarled up with debris. The rain continued for two more days. The creek water levels rose and rose to eight metres high and a hundred metres across. Whole trees were being uprooted and whizzed down the rapids, along with the odd car too! Sadly, some animals were caught off guard – a few sheep with bloated bellies, legs in the air swirled past.

The pattern of sixty to eighty millimetres in the morning and then again in the evening repeated itself. Cid was constantly texting Steve to ask how much rain we'd got, although the signal was intermittent and so the texting was erratic. Cid was elated by the rains, that much was clear. He texts said, 'Won't need to destock now.' 'We're right for a good few years yet, eh?'

Even after the rain had stopped for a few days, there was no way on or off the station. All ground was boggy, meaning no vehicle could pass. It would be another week, if not weeks, depending on the weather, before we could venture out into the soft-scoop dog poop of ground.

Naturally, I had time for writing, and while Steve busied himself with jobs in the shed, after I'd done my bit around the house, I opened up Locked in One Nest and moved the story along.

> When complaints are made about Alia's poor teaching, she's told to take time off. She uses the opportunity to see Catherine, Mark's mother, who said to her, about a year ago, 'Beware Mark.' Alia needs to know how Mark's first wife, Amelia, died. Catherine, in a shock reveal, tells her it was from 'an unexplained and fatal heart attack'. Alia wants to go to the police but Catherine forbids it, saying Mark's father, David, vehemently denies any suggestion that Mark was connected to Amelia's death and would punish her if Alia goes to the police. Plus, there is no longer proof. Amelia was cremated, precluding any post-mortem toxicology examination.

I started writing the dialogue and it was like it was coming from somewhere else. When I stopped, I found I didn't want to stop and started a new chapter summary.

> Alia returns home determined to have a private investigator examine Mark's dark research and compile a dossier of the compromising research into poisons that will prove his malintent. However, when Alia goes into Mark's study again, everything is gone – both the laptop and the newspaper clipping on the murdering dentist. She has nothing to give to a PI. What she does do is abort the baby and throw Mark out of the house. Then she makes an appointment with a good divorce lawyer. However, she is now aware that if Mark found out about the abortion, her life would be in danger, which is exactly what happens, and once again Alia fears for her life at Mark's hands.

Good, it was coming along nicely. Wouldn't be long before I was sending it off to an agent, and I knew just which one.

# Mud, Devastation and the Clean-up Operation

We began waking up to bright sunshine and, before long, the ground had dried out enough to merit a recce mission. There were some gruesome sights. A big ram was stuck in the parted tree trunks of a gum, its long weighty testicles hanging down like they were ripe for target practice – Steve's observation. The pipe that fed Bedlam tank was broken. Steve wouldn't be able to get to it until the waters in the front creek had subsided completely. It wasn't urgent to fix because the sheep don't go to the troughs when they have water in the meadows and pastures. However, we would be losing a lot of water in other parts of Amirda where Steve hadn't been able to shut off the tanks. It would be a few more days before we could risk taking the vehicle out. Cid advised that we 'Wait till the creek has dried out completely.' That was good advice that we, Steve, did not follow.

We watched the water levels drop and drop and Steve declared the creek had dried up enough to venture out. My heart sank. I didn't want to go out there. We went for a walkabout down to the main creek.

I breathed in and my nose was full of something horrible. 'What stinks?' I asked Steve.

He said it would be the ram stuck in the tree. 'Though it could be other dead animals,' he said, shrugging.

Walking over to the ute, we saw that the ground was a mixture of soft and hard but Steve said it was good enough and, after all, there were fences that needed fixing and pipes putting back together. I think Steve was worried about how many stray sheep he was going to have to round up alone on the motorbike.

I pictured the outback looking like Salvador Dali's painting of melted watch faces draped over parched tree branches with rocky cliffs in the distance. I thought, if we do get out there, we would spend the day in scorching heat picking up broken fencing, and sifting through mud-sodden detritus. Plus, we'd be in isolated corners where, if we got stuck, we couldn't walk back and no one could know we were there – that's if we didn't stumble across some fugitive hiding out with his gun. I groaned inwardly. I was too ashamed to tell Steve how I was feeling. He was anxious about what was out there for him to have to put right. But my anxiety about venturing into the remote paddocks was so strong, my chest hurt.

'What's up?' asked Steve, frowning hard, as I was getting into the ute.

I gave him a big grin and said, 'Nothing. Looking forward to getting out at last.'

He relaxed and smiled back as he backed out of the garage, then started talking excitedly about what we should expect to find. 'A lot of broken pipes and ripped open fencing,' was his prediction.

I had to look away to show my real emotions – a grimace into the distance.

We didn't get far along the road to Camel-foe before we got bogged. I wanted to smack him in the ear. A blind lunatic could see the ground was too soft even for the four-wheel drive. Steve had to walk all the way back to the homestead to fetch the tractor to pull us out. I didn't like being left there, but no way I was walking all that distance in mud. As he walked off, I looked around at the many fallen tree trunks, like giant ivory tusks scattered about. The creek bed gave the impression of an elephant graveyard. I sat back and tried to think of Locked in One Nest, and what Alia's next move would be.

Shrieks of noise overhead jolted me. I looked up to see the pink underbellies of a flock of galahs. They came to land in the trees and on the ground – like the cockatoos, they seemed to travel and communicate in pairs, squawking to each other, perhaps to keep together, who knows. The birds felt like company, the good kind.

I turned on the radio – just the one channel, ABC for South Australia. I was trying to tell myself I wasn't nervous about being alone. The radio program was a phone-in talkback show. Farmers and pastoralists were calling in to share their experiences of having rain after years of drought. You could hear their joy and relief. In contrast, some people were ringing in to talk about how they had lost their house or animals because of the bushfires. One woman broke down as she told of having to leave a field full of cattle to burn alive, and now the dry heat and the fires were back and she was worried all over again. Her traumatised voice brought tears to my eyes. What a country of contrasts Australia was!

Yet I was feeling that I wasn't part of any of it, their joy or despair. I was caught in other people's lives. This wasn't my drama. I wasn't a pastoralist, or even a caretaker. I wasn't even a resident or planning to stay married to my Aussie husband. I didn't want to be in the outback – I didn't even think I wanted to be in the country. I certainly didn't want to go on this water run with Steve if we ever got the ute out of the mud. It was a depressing feeling, the kind that you feel in your gut, like love sickness. This must be some sort of life sickness, or it was so at that despairing time, while I waited for Steve for hours and hours.

The news came on. More about the growing cases of Covid. I'd seen all this in Saudi with MERS (Middle East respiratory syndrome) and also SARS, whatever that one stood for, but it was a respiratory syndrome virus anyway. Why was everyone panicking over this strain?

Over two hours later, Steve chugged up on the tractor.

I said, 'Are you towing me back?'

He said, 'No! We're going out to assess the damage, I told you.'

He was making us go out and risk getting bogged again and again. Was he going to follow me in the tractor all the way to Mount Remote? It would take us until midnight – oh, and he'd probably run out of fuel. Why wasn't he making any sense?

He hooked up a towrope and got back in the driver's seat of the tractor. He pulled me and the ute out, only for us to get stuck again.

Steve looked back and shouted, 'For fuck's sake, you have to drive out of the mud not into it!'

I started to shake with anger. Fuck it. Fuck the consequences. Fuck Steve! I got out of the ute and slammed the door so hard it could have busted the lock. The force I used caused me to stagger back. I lost a boot to the deep mud. I tried to remain upright on one leg and turned to pull my boot out of the mud, but I fell on my arse. I screamed with frustration and punched the ground. Mud splattered in my face and I burst into tears and sat sobbing, face down turned away from Steve. Steve came towards me, holding the tow rope. I looked up, swore at him, and thought, I don't care if you finish me off – go on, kill me. I hate myself anyway.

He said, 'You look like someone farted diarrhoea on your face.'

I don't know how, but it made me laugh – a lot.

He held out his hand and pulled me up. 'Let's see what Camel-foe is like, then we'll go back, I promise,' said Steve, wiping my face with his sleeve.

# Will the Crows or Eagles Eat Us First?

Steve saw sense and we didn't go out in the ute for two more days. It was wonderful to see how green and lustrous the paddocks and mountains had become. The land had been transformed. I imagined the starved sheep gorging themselves on sweet saltbush, if saltbush can be sweet. Perhaps sweet is a figure of speech.

I went back to my novel. Steve was no longer making literary life difficult for me by being so very nice. Mark now had a character all his own. I got back into it and wrote up the next part, which went,

> At the prestigious gala dinner held at their university, Alia and Mark have to share a table. They have a public show of marital discord and the evening finishes with a grand-scale humiliation of Mark that was posted on social media by his former star pupil, Miley Hooley, who was expelled for plagiarism. Miley has been spying on Mark, secretly taping his sexual transgressions. She was also blackmailing him to give her a place at university; but, when he failed to secure her degree, she took her revenge.
>
> Three days later, Mark Dunn is found dead in his office. He's been poisoned to death. The last meal he ate is likely to have been at the gala dinner. At one point Alia, by mistake (we think,) had Mark's dinner served to her. She was seen to empty the contents of a sachet of salt over it before returning the dinner to Mark. While awaiting the toxicology report, Alia is under suspicion for the murder of her husband. Miley Hooley is another suspect – they are the only two.

I remember thinking, 'I feel so much better now that Mark is dead. What power a writer has. If only it were as easy to control the actual world. Some people seem to have that power, certainly not me.' I didn't want to kill Steve, of course, but sometimes I just wished he'd go away and leave me be. I believe many partners wish this of the other. Alas, it's hardly ever mutual – wouldn't that save a lot of murders!

A few days later, it was safe to venture out. The hot sun had done its job and the rains were truly history. Steve and I had to study the main map of the property in the office to mark which fences to prioritise. It was likely that every fence that crossed a creek would be down. Some we might be able to pull up and restore, others would have to be completely replaced, which would involve taking the tractor out. I had to help Steve – it would take forever to do on his own. Cid was already getting calls from neighbouring pastoralists who were furious because Amirda's dorpers were mixing with whoever's merinos. The fact that Cid had switched from merino sheep to dorpers had been a major source of neighbourly discord until Cid put up dorper-proof fencing. In the past, the inadequate fencing had led to out and out feuding as cross-breeding weakened the merino wool. Lawsuits had been served over old-fence disputes and grudges were still held by some. Cid would say it was so-and-so's responsibility to erect a suitable fence, or any fence, and they would say it was his.

One such disputed fence was out west at Mount Remote where it shared a boundary with the BM station, the station we had to cross through those gates, where I still believed a poacher to be hiding out in the drover's cottage with no roof on. I called the BM station after the Bates Motel because the pastoralist there ran station stays and, to me, the set up was totally Norman Bates from Hitchcock's movie Psycho. The guy even looked like the deranged son Norman who murders the guests who stay at his hotel.

I would get to see more of the BM than I cared to but that's for a bit later. The point here, regarding the fences, was that the Pastoralist Board had decreed in favour of Cid, and so it was not El Cid's responsibility to mend the fence that separated his property from Norman's. Cid had paid for and erected the current fence using Amirda's labour, but thereafter, it was Norman's responsibility for some stipulation in the bargain I forget. It had to do with the board trying to be fair to both parties and blah blah blah, it doesn't matter, you get the picture. The point was, the maintenance of the fence was now Norman's responsibility. That was generally how things went down in these parts. It was all about trade-offs, negotiations and so forth. Very feudal England as far as I could see. However, it had been over six years since any creeks had flowed and so this was fertile ground for disputes again – those sitting on the Pastoralist Board wouldn't even be the same people who presided over the last squabbles. Consequently, station owners were disagreeing about who was responsible for what. It probably didn't help that some agreements had been settled with a spit and a handshake in Copley pub!

I was rejoicing that we wouldn't have to go out to Mount Remote and assess the BM fence, but another text from Cid said, 'Go have a look to see if the cunt's put it back up.'

We set off with water, lunch and snacks for an entire day. Who knew when we'd get back? It wouldn't be until dark.

However, on the way there, we hit a hurdle. We could not pass under the disused Ghan rail track because the tunnels under it were flooded. That meant going over the track but the sleepers were set high on gravel and then there were the iron rails to get over. As Steve drove up the hill to see the rail, I feared we might get stuck, buckle a wheel or damage the chassis. We got out and tried to shore up the approach as best we could. Steve was determined to get across. We did, after much jolting about. On inspection, the ute didn't appear fatigued. Toyotas are tanks! Just as well because the vehicle had to plough through and get around the devastation around us – namely, fallen fences, huge banks of muddy debris, and fallen trees. Sheep were scattered far and wide, many on the wrong property – binoculars confirmed sheep were mixing. The merino farmers would be hopping mad that thin-coated dorpers were mingling and breeding with their fine woolly stock.

One beautiful novelty was the appearance of a lake on what was before dry land. The pop-up waterhole already had an abundance of wildlife: ducks with chicks, geese and black swans tootled around like they'd been there for ever. We stopped the car and had a long look at the delightful sight through the circle of low trees. We would see a few such natural wonders over the course of the week.

But we soon had to get back to work. When we reached the BM fence that crossed the creek, we saw that, sure enough, it had been ripped wide open and remained ripped wide open with no signs of anyone coming to pick it back up.

'Shit,' said Steve,. 'This probably means I'll have to do it now.'

There was phone signal because the Telstra tower was nearby on top of one of the mountain peaks. Steve sent off his text and we walked the fence line to see what could be salvaged. I continued to keep an eye out for poachers, but the place showed no signs of tyre tracks or footprints, so we were safe. There were, however, hoof prints – of cattle not sheep. We couldn't see any cows but they were definitely on Amirda land. There had been a mass exodus out of the BM. Steve shook his head.

A text came back from Cid. 'Yeah, get it back up but take pictures of before and after so I can bill the…'

There were a lot of expletives added but I don't need to share them.

Much of the fence was mangled around tree roots or branches. Steve didn't want to bring the tractor all this way to roll out an entirely new fence, so we were determined to get the old one back up. It involved a lot of excavation work and muscle. Flies began darting at my face and buzzing in my ears, so I put my flynet on. Steve said he couldn't see properly with his flynet so I had to put up with his swearing non-stop as flies drank from his sweaty face. Gloves on, we went further into the creek to begin the rest of the fence-recovery operation. I reminded Steve to take a picture of the sorry scene.

Some of the fence was so twisted up as to be impossible to unpick. Some of it was wrapped tightly around the roots and branches of a colossal gum tree. Most of the gum trees were in a sorry state, their silvery brown bark hanging off in strips, their roots exposed by as much as two meters, like those at Amirda Creek.

'Are these exposed trees more prone to falling in the softer mud?' I asked Steve, and he gave me a sarcastic, 'We might find out shortly.'

I swallowed nervously as I bent down and started seeing what I could shake loose with my fingers, then I'd use a hand fork, then a rake, all the time trying to keep one eye on the gum tree for signs of tipping, and one ear alert for sounds of a breaking branch. Salvaging a fence from a mud avalanche is almost like an archaeological dig. It is painstaking, dirty work, pulling away at fencing wire mangled up with soil, twigs, branches, leaves, bark and long gnarly root systems.

Pulling at a section that was lost in the mud, I stuck my hand in further to see if it would come lose, then – 'Whoa, shit…' a giant millipede scurried out and disappeared into a hole in my ankle boot – or did it? I scrambled up to shake my boot off. I felt crushing pain. I screamed and Steve came running.

'I think I've been bitten,' I yelped, pulling off my boot, holding onto Steve.

It turned out to be a spiny bindi from the crawler plants on the ground. It had got caught between my heel and boot. I pulled it free and it pierced my finger, drawing blood. It had felt like something sinking its teeth into my flesh. The millipede was nowhere to be seen, thank God.

Drama over, I got back to raking the soil off the wire and was soon able to shake off the rest and wrench up a section of fence. But something else jumped on me and I was screaming again. Steve stood up and rolled his eyes at my hysterics.

I shouted, 'It's alive and green and it's on me.' I was doing a dance to rid myself of something deadly before it could drop into my exposed open boot and give me a deadly bite. I saw in a flash why Cid wore his trouser legs rolled down over his boots.

It was soon Steve's turn to yell out and have me running over to him. I saw him throwing something. It turned out that he'd grabbed a baby snake, which, luckily for him, he'd picked up around the throat so that it couldn't turn its head and bite him – at least that was Steve's guess as he threw the thing far into the creek. These are the kinds of distractions that keep you from crapping your pants about trees falling on you or dying of dehydration when you realise you didn't bring enough water and there's still half a day of backbreaking work ahead of you.

When we finally got the fence free, we pulled what we could into place. Now we had to roll out the replacement fencing. It took some effort to get the roll from the ute. I helped as best I could to steady the bulky cylinder of hard wire as Steve unrolled it along the ground. This was only part of a full roll of fencing. A full one is impossible to handle – you need a tractor and its prong for that. Then the new steel droppers needed to be put in place. We weren't able to salvage many of the existing ones – they were bent double in the ground. Some Steve pulled out, but they had to be taken back for a cut and weld. He had brought a collection of droppers which were in the ute. But he couldn't hammer some of them into the ground because it was too rocky. Then some were the wrong length and I'd have to go back to the ute and get a shorter one.

When we finally got the fence up, it was too wobbly and needed straining to stay upright. The strainer was in two parts and looked like it came from the eighteenth century. It was two heavy iron chains with what looked like a fish head attached to its end. It took an hour for Steve to work out how to make it strain a fence but eventually he got the thing connecting and pulling the fence upright.

Then Steve needed more wire cut to prepare for the tie-ups. 'No, the soft wire,' he said when I came back with the wrong loop.

I was running between him and the ute almost non-stop, fetching and carrying tools and kit. To and fro, over rocks and broken branches. I'd be as lean as the wire when it was over!

Finally, we were all done. Looking at the completed fence, we both felt great satisfaction. Steve took another picture and sent the before and after shots to Cid, who would no doubt negotiate some return favour or charge from Norman for our – sorry, 'his' – labour. But it was hard to believe that we had only just started the fence recovery operation of a place the size of Snowdonia. We had about forty more to go! It would take weeks, but the pressure was on to get it done quickly and get the sheep back to where they belonged – Steve back on his bike, driving them through the correct gate. So, without further ado, as they say, we were off to the next creek and then the next, guzzling water and slapping more sunscreen on the back of our necks.

As midday approached, I was overheated and so was Steve. His cheeks were scorched red with effort and sunburn. I told him he wasn't drinking enough water, but then I saw that we hadn't brought enough to last the two of us for the day. I suggested returning to the homestead and coming back out later when it was cooler. Steve pointed out that the days don't actually get cooler, and in fact get hotter into the evening. But when he said, about returning for more water, 'Nah, we'll be right,' I thought, maybe after all we will end up as bleached carcasses in the blistering sun just like that kangaroo and emu we encountered on our first journey into Amirda. At lunch, I ate my tuna sandwiches hoping the cucumber would provide a much-needed source of water.

Soon we were on to another fence. I forced myself into robot mode – just keep on, fixing one tangled mess after another, and the fences were coming up faster and faster. Steve, I will hand it to him, worked like four men to my one. At last, we were driving out to what I hoped would be the last fence of the day. But the droppers weren't going into the ground as they should – the rocks were too solid and Steve kept having to find another spot to hammer then in. I felt sorry for his shoulder, which he was increasingly having to massage to help with the pain.

Crows began to fly overhead and roost in the high gum tree canopies directly above us. It was as though they were watching us. Their rasping exchanges seemed to be getting more excited as more and more crows gathered in the trees and looked down at our slow progress. They sounded like toothless witches with their maniacal cries. A murder of crows. Scavengers of death. It was definitely us they were looking at and getting excited about. Steve looked up and saw how many they were. He bent down, picked up a rock and threw it at them, swearing. They kept up their mad chorus. I swear those crows were inviting family and friends to come be the first to dine on these two red-faced gringos who looked fit to drop any minute. I was even more worried when two massive wedgetail eagles began circling above the crows. Could they smell that we were turning into carrion?

As well as the noise of the crows and menace of the eagles, I was always looking around for snakes, scorpions and millipedes, or looking up at the lower gum tree overhangs, praying one wouldn't rip away and break my back in two, especially now that a fierce wind had kicked up and was forcing the bushy canopies to bounce about violently.

Hours later, Steve had got all the droppers fixed in place and strained the fence in place. We stood back to look at the great long fence back up over the rocky creek bed. I could not quite believe we were finished. I dabbed the now empty water bottle spout on my tongue while he loaded the last of the unused wire and droppers in the tray of the ute.

I said, 'Finally, it's home time.'

To which Steve informed me that we could fit in one more fence.

'We've got no water left, Steve. It's not possible to carry on working and live.'

He came around and picked up a khaki jerry can, saying, 'Emergency water supplies.'

'That's old water. We'll get legionnaire's disease,' I protested.

He assured me that he'd swilled it out and refilled it that morning. I might have had a hissy-fit breakdown there and then if I hadn't been distracted by a group of merinos. They ran off in the opposite direction as soon as they saw us.

Steve said, 'They were probably trying to get back through the fence. They're stuck on our side now.'

What the hell, I had to drink something. I went to pick up the jerrycan but then I heard a new noise that sounded like a cow. No, it was louder. I turned around and saw a bull standing there, head down. I gave out a whimper and Steve came running, making big claps with his hands and the beast ran off. I scrambled into the ute.

Steve joined me and promised that after one more fence, we'd be done. Mercifully, it took less than an hour and we were at last heading back. There was a final drama to the day – those cinnamon horses from Urdlu were roaming on Amirda land. Now there were both cattle and horses to round up as well as sheep. Happy days!

## What is Covid?

About day four into the fence fixes, we came across the guys who owned TC Station. We wanted to speak to them about their merinos which were now roaming on Amirda lands – no hassle, just the way it was. Of course, they too would tell us they had spotted Cid's dorpers. I called the guy Eastwood because he was tall, handsome and laconic, with a smile that made your face light up. Eastwood didn't notice us approaching because his electric driver machine was making so much noise. Steve couldn't wait to see exactly what the contraption was. Here was a driver gadget to make fence fixing a whole lot easier. Zap, zap, zap – dropper in, no sweat on brow.

As we were getting out of the ute, we saw his wife, Bella. She was petite and slender but with the strength of a man. She was carrying a boulder I don't think I could lift. She placed the huge stone on the wire fencing where it met the ground. You had to do it at uneven parts of the fence line to stop animals from getting underneath.

Like her husband, she was super friendly and shook my hand with warmth, saying, 'How yuz going?'

Steve told her that he wanted to take a picture of the driver machine.

Eastwood told Steve to send it to Cid right away. 'Should have one of these to save your back and shoulders.'

Steve did so.

I thought, so you think you're going to be here for another bout of fence fixing, hey, Steve? I vowed to myself that I would not be around for the next rains.

We then got on to the topic of the stray merinos and dorpers. Steve and Eastwood decided to meet up on their bikes to do a round-up later that day. We ended up having a cup of tea with Eastwood and Bella. Eastwood made a little fire from leaves and twigs and placed an old fashioned billy on the pile to boil the water. They were real bush people, and I loved them for their friendliness. There had been friction in the past with Cid and his dorpers but that was between the elders – Eastwood and Bella were having none of it and wanted to get along with their neighbours. They insisted on sharing their smoko cake with us too.

It took over two weeks of non-stop work to get the fences sorted. Cid came up with an electric driver contraption and helped Steve do the last of the fences. He also stayed on to help Steve and Eastwood muster the rest of the sheep, cattle and horses that were proving stubborn to get back in. I was free to finish my book. I had to read back what I'd written, to work out how Alia was going to get free of blame for Mark's murder.

> A blow to Alia's credibility comes when she tells police that Mark may have been involved in his first wife's death. The chief inspector in charge of Mark's murder investigation informs Alia that Mark's first wife died of ovarian cancer, not a heart attack. What is more, Catherine, Mark's mother, has paranoid schizophrenia and has wrongly accused her son of killing his wife, since she saw an article in the newspaper about a dentist who murdered his wives (this she sent to Mark). By telling the police all this, Alia only shows she had a lot of reasons to be scared of Mark and therefore a strong motive for murdering him.

While I was thinking through the resolution to the novel, I looked at the calendar and realised that our three-month stint was nearing its end. I had almost forgotten that staying at Amirda was not a life sentence. I thought, Never again will I have to pull up a broken fence, dodge deadly snakes or clean a slimy trough.

I did a little shuffle dance around the office, singing, 'We are leaving, we are leaving, start the engines, start the engines…fire fire, fire fire…' I stopped there and hoped we wouldn't get trapped in any late summer bush fires. Mustn't tempt fate. There were still a few issues with the Bus, but Steve had been fixing it steadily the whole time and there was nothing major.

A week later, we were waiting for El Cid to come with the replacement caretaker. Steve and I had cleared out the bedroom and bathroom of our stuff. The Bus was packed up, and fuelled up thanks to Cid's generosity – he allowed us to use the diesel pump at Amirda. We had booked a stay at Port Pirie and then would travel to Adelaide, where we would sell the Bus. Steve had agreed that once we sold the van, I could buy an air ticket and go see my mother – oh, it was on, folks, this time on a jet plane. He also agreed that there was no need for him to go to the UK with me. It was all 'too easy', as the Aussies say, meaning 'all good', in case you're not familiar. Steve would go see his brothers in Victoria and decide what to do with the rest of his life. Not that he was aware of just how much he'd have to readjust. I was happy that there would be no need for a dramatic split. Once home, I would simply tell him I wasn't coming back to Australia.

Another beautiful bonus about leaving Amirda was that I had finished my psychological thriller. These were the last of the notes that I would write up:

> Alia descends into a vortex of confusion as she tries to make sense of how Mark is dead and she is number-one suspect. The reader is left wondering if Alia is involved. After all, she wanted rid of Mark and saw no easy way out. She felt that he would forever be a thorn in her side unless something drastic happened. Plus, she is not good at facing her own reality.

I wrote the end of the mystery with what I felt to be great mastery. Now I had to send it to the highest literary agent in London. Sofia (let's call her that) had been waiting for something really good from me for a long time.

I did a covering letter to Sofia, attached the first three chapters with this synopsis:

> Locked in One Nest is a psychological thriller about a wife's struggle to escape her controlling husband. It's about Alia's fight to silence the voice that says her dark suspicions are groundless and free the spirit that screams Mark is a controlling sociopath

who she needs to get the hell away from. The question is, how far will she go to get Mark away from her? Finally, there is the deeply troubled student, Miley. Her edgy narrative is woven through the novel and reveals details about Alia's marriage that Alia herself can't or won't tell us.

Miley – I wasn't sure about this character. I don't know where her voice came from. Perhaps it was the inner me, crude, mean and mentally ill through enforced solitude – if I can self-diagnose correctly. In some ways, Miley was the only real character in the novel. I prayed Sofia would like her but feared Miley wasn't everyone's cup of tea. Well, time would tell – the email was sent. I did, however have the sudden conviction that I had not written a crowd-pleaser with the Miley character. Whatever, it was too late for misgivings.

I tried not to take it as a bad sign when Steve came back to the house without the Bus and said, 'I can't get it to start.'

'You charged up the battery, didn't you?'

'Yeah, both of them, but we got a major oil leak now that I thought I'd fixed. That will have to be sorted before we can drive it out of here.'

The sound of Cid's ute coming over the creek put an end to the conversation, but I wasn't worried – if Steve couldn't fix the oil leak, Cid sure would be able to.

We went out to meet him. I was surprised when I saw there was no car following behind. But perhaps the caretaker guy was coming later that day or later in the week. Cid got out. He looked tired and wasn't his usual ebullient self, shouting some cheery nonsense at us. Instead, he got out and leant against the car door after shaking hands with Steve in a gloomy manner. He took his hat off and put it to his chest. He was so quiet. Of course, he was upset because we were leaving. Bless, I was touched.

'How's things?' I asked, attempting to inject some cheerfulness into the gloomy atmosphere.

He put his hat back on. 'Ah, things are good with me, but not with the country, eh? They've declared a national emergency.'

Steve and I looked at each other.

'What's going on in the country?' I asked. This was Cid's silly joke because he knew how desperate I was to leave. I'd heard Steve talking to him about how we couldn't stay on because of how, me, the city girl was going stir-crazy out in the sticks, plus, and this was the best to hear coming from Steve: 'She's going back to England for a month or two.'

'You haven't heard?' said Cid, shaking his head and grimacing. 'All flights are grounded and borders are closing at midnight – tonight. Country is shutting down because of the Covid pandemic.'

'You mean, I can't leave the country and go to England?' I asked. And even though I'd asked the question, I didn't believe it could be the case. It sounded like he said all the borders were closing, but that wasn't possible, was it?

'We'll put the news on. See the latest,' he said, walking up to the house.

The next hour was taken up with hearing all the news we had missed. We only listened to news on water-run days and then not always if Steve put his music on. Steve had his music on a lot the last weeks. It was true that Australia was closing its international borders and the states looked to be closing theirs too. We were all going into periods of lockdown. Still, we were leaving, I said to myself.

'The new guy isn't coming now in case he can't get back to Victoria…' Cid kept talking but I was too stunned to take it in.

At that point, I was still hopeful that Steve and I would leave at the end of the week. I refused to listen to pessimistic forecasts and Cid's overtures of 'You're welcome to stay on here as long as you like.' We were going, mate. Make no mistake. The situation wouldn't last, it would be over within a month, for sure. Cid would have to come and babysit the sheep himself.

The next day, Cid was back to his usual happy self at breakfast, but when he said, 'Any red sauce?' as I was placing sausages on the table, I could have chucked the ketchup bottle at him.

I sat down but didn't have a plate in front of me. It was clear I didn't want breakfast.

He said, 'All good, all good – ladies can have a diet shake, I know all about your diet shakes.'

I didn't know what the hell he was talking about. I picked up my tea and felt I could cry.

Cid began telling Steve that he was having his Broken Hill cattle trucked to the BM. 'You'll come up there with me?' he asked and Steve said, 'Sure.'

Then Cid was telling Steve about how he would see how his cattle fared in the BM paddocks and perhaps a muster in a few months.

Steve made some joke about 'You've patched things up with Norman then?' and Cid frowned like he didn't even know what Steve was referring to. No doubt Cid's cattle were going to be fed in payment for putting up that boundary fence.

It was business as usual in so many ways. Cid joking with me about being on a diet was just him trying to brush over the deception he and Steve were playing on me. Both men were behaving unnaturally. I suspected too that there was no oil leak in the Bus – Steve would have picked up on that before. Maybe Steve even knew about the imminent border closures and was keeping it from me so that I didn't bolt sooner.

Then Cid spoke to me. 'I got some relatives stopping by today, but we'll be up at BM. It's just a quick visit from my cousin's family – they used to play here as kids, and want to have a look at the place. You'll give them some tea and scones?'

'What?' I was on the verge of tears.

Cid smiled gently at me. 'Sorry, my bad, that was a joke, no need to bake anything, but can you give them a cup of tea and a biscuit?'

'Yes,' I said, unable to keep the fatigue out of my voice.

When they left for the BM, and after I'd cleared away breakfast, I took out flour and butter. I would make scones. I had to do something. I got some double cream out of the freezer. I would do the whole English thing and we'd have something to talk about and stop me from having a seizure. But the tears were coming at the prospect of spending God only knew how much more time on the station. Steve would persuade me to stay on with him because it would be too fricken difficult for me to venture off on my own. He was already talking in defeatist terms. 'Don't suppose it would be so bad to do another few months. We can save money.'

I sat on the veranda to wait for Cid's cousins. My Devonshire cream tea was on the kitchen table waiting for the guests. No, it was Dorpershire cream tea. I tried to smile at my pun.

A roaring noise jolted me from my thoughts. That wasn't just the trees, windy as it was. I looked for the plumes of dust, but saw nothing. Trees were bending and swirling – it was the wind. I saw sheep heading in from different directions, following the lines they make called pads. They would start to run the last leg. I saw some running, just as I had predicted and it brought a little smile to my face. I did like dorper sheep, sheep full-stop, gentle, amiable creatures.

A car, two cars were coming – there was the dust in the air. El Cid's cousins were arriving.

'I'd better put the kettle on,' I said, wiping tears out of my eyes.

However, my phone pinged. It was my Gmail, which meant one thing: Sofia had already got back to me. Was it good or bad? I read her email, and kept reading the same line over and over, which said, 'Yes, this looks promising, do send the rest of Locked in One Nest if you have finished the full manuscript.'

I ran inside, and quicky opened my laptop. I would send the entire novel there and then. As Cid's guests approached, I was attaching Locked in One Nest to a reply email. When I pressed the send button, I said a little prayer: 'Please, Sofia, God, Goddesses, love my novel and get it published, and get me out of here.' I looked out of the window at the posse of travellers getting out of their cars. I smiled, now without having to fake it.

A month later, when I hadn't heard from Sofia, I sent an email to see if she had received the novel, and if so, what were her thoughts – a month was a long time for her. She got back to me that same day. I read her email expecting to see 'This looked promising but I'm afraid...' et cetera. But no. She had only sent an agency agreement contract! She loved the novel. I had to read her words over and over to make sure I wasn't mistaken. She said she had sent me an email. I certainly hadn't had one, but no matter. Thank God I'd got in touch was all I could think. I became an OMG screeching wreck of a thing, singing, 'Sofia is going to represent my book. I will be published. We are talking bestseller lists!' It was over – my trailing around after Steve, my giving up good lecturing and teaching jobs for nothing but an uncertain future… I had finally won!

# Part Two

# Stuck on the Station

Eight months later, I didn't feel so much like a winner. I had heard nothing good from Sofia. I'd sent two emails asking her how my novel was faring with the buyers, but there was no bidding war, nothing like it – there was not even any interest at this stage. But London was in lockdown, agents were furloughed at home, and I just had to be patient.

One good thing was that I now had a few pets, two blue-tongued lizards to be precise (some call them skinks). They were a pair and would do a circuit of the veranda most days. At first, they would hiss at me, poking out their tongues, like the wild ones on the water run, but they began coming to the window, whereupon I would get some lettuce and cucumber for them, and a drink. So they became pets. I got some good video footage of them doing their funny walk around the place.

I was doing lots of birdwatching too, and growing tomatoes. I was also into creating pots of jams and chutneys from all the fruits the orchard trees produced: finger limes, plums, mandarins, berries and figs. Then there were all the oranges, lemons fruiting in abundance – Steve had a good irrigation system going. Amirda even had a quandong tree. I didn't even know what quandongs were, although there were many Quandong cafés along the Flinders.

The fruit is a species of wild native peach dating back forty million years, real bush tucker, and excellent for preserving, and doubtless has infinite uses I'll never know about. Steve and I had assumed the red berries were poisonous and let them rot on the tree and ground (shame on us). Yet no birds seemed interested in them. The cockatoos stripped the gum trees of their leaves but they didn't eat fruit that I could see. The crows got into the orange tree but that was about it. Anyway, I ended up with a whole cupboard full of quandong jam and chutney, along with a whole host of other preserves in jars.

Talking of which, Steve had his own distractions, namely rearranging the various storage containers and bottles in the kitchen. I'd walk in from feeding my blue-tongues to find him arranging the plethora of tea, coffee and sugar pots so that they appeared in order of ascending height. Then he would move on to the oil bottles, of which there was a growing collection: olive oils, mushroom oils, nut oils – all gifts from El Cid's visitors that he and his wife won't eat or use. It was getting like that film Sleeping with the Enemy with Julia Roberts. The tins in the cupboards were stacked as if they were on a supermarket display shelf. I imagined myself living some place that Steve didn't know about. I'm enjoying my messy cupboards and disorderly home, but one day I open a cupboard to see cans of beans et cetera in hideous rows of symmetry. He found me!

'There, that's better,' said Steve, nodding at the neat row of jars. He was turning into Mark from Locked in One Nest! He didn't make a joke along the lines of 'I know, I'm anal' like he used to. That meant he was pissed off. Oh, of course he was, because I wouldn't blow him or have sex. I can't, I just can't and I don't care how cranky he gets. Well, I do, but I can't help him.

If I got up to put my cup in the sink and he was walking that way, he would do an about turn and walk the other way around the table. The footwork was military-like. He was changing the guard at Buckingham Palace. Not being able to pass each other in the kitchen was a new source of irritation in our domestic confinement over a very long winter. If I went to the sink or kettle and he too was on his way to that spot, he'd say, 'No, sorry, you go first.' It was all I could do not to scream, it doesn't fucking matter if we pass each other.

Even more stressful, if I showed my frustration, he'd say, 'Oops, don't upset the Mrs,' like I was the psycho! I wanted to lash out at his head or stab him in the neck with the butter knife, but to show any signs of irritation made for an explosive argument where he'd throw his arms up and rave about 'just trying to be respectful of your space' or some crap I couldn't relate to. I really didn't feel safe having arguments when we were so isolated. For most of the winter, we had seen nothing of Cid, nothing of anyone. At Leigh Creek, only one of us was allowed in the store, so of course, Steve did the shopping. For all I knew, his brain could be getting weird. The TV was reporting an epidemic of domestic violence episodes in the Covid lockdowns. Covid, Covid… I did not know how much longer I could last.

Run, I needed to run, go for a real run, as far as I could go. I was getting fat and, contrasted to Steve's trimness, it was unbearable. There were too many fat jokes around now too, and probably Steve did not find me so attractive. He is very sizeist. Yet Steve's insistence on three meals a day was the culprit, although he laughed at the idea, saying I must be a secret eater. Not so. Marriage is what makes people like me fat. I have to eat when I'm not hungry, it's too stressful not to. I tried it at the beginning of our marriage and it didn't work. He refused to eat too and it became a thing, so it was easier just to do the three meals a day and avoid the 'No, I'll support you. We're in this together,' followed by an evening of irritable scowl syndrome.

Well, I would run the damn fat off me. Amirda had so much space for it. The scenery was stunning and I had so much time. I only needed to stop being a wuss about venturing out there alone. Yes, I could run myself as trim as scoffing Stevo.

I went to the bedroom and got out my runners, leggings and a vest top. I did some stretching to get me in the mood, and I was good to go.

'Jesus, what's this – fancy dress?' said Steve as I was stepping out of the house.

'Yes. I am going to jog every day.' I smiled, challenging him to ridicule my intentions.

'Take plenty of water. And don't take this the wrong way, but you're very out of shape. Don't want you collapsing with heatstroke.'

Well, at least he didn't laugh at me, but it was a shame he couldn't be helpful without being mean. But if I pulled him up, he'd say it was just banter and I shouldn't be so touchy.

'Yeah, thanks, I did forget my water,' I said as cheerfully as I could. No point getting into a row. I needed him on my side as much as he was able to be.

'Where you going to run to?' he asked, following me into the house.

'I'll go all the way to Bedlam. Half hour there, half hour back, so be back in an hour.'

I took out the water from the fridge and when I turned around, he was right in front of me.

'You're really going all that way on your own? Not afraid you'll be shot by the roo shooters?' He smiled.

Was this becoming a war of attrition? Well, he wasn't going to wear me down. I had fight enough in me.

'Not afraid of roo shooters at all. I'm over that silliness. Now move aside, there's a good chap.' I wanted to push him out of the way.

He stood aside, saying, 'I'll be in the butcher's room when you get back.'

'The what?'

'The abattoir, cold-room, whatever it's called, the one just out the back here. Cid asked me if I wouldn't mind cleaning it up. Cid didn't give Norman all of his cattle back. There were some on an outer paddock at Mount Remote and Cid told me to leave them. So we might be eating Bates Motel steaks soon.'

I had no idea if the story was true, but it was good that he was lightening up. We had to lighten up, both of us. I know I'm attacking Steve a lot here. It was difficult to get a clear perspective sometimes. Perhaps I was bugging the shit out of him more than I knew, with my hatred of being at the station. But I was trying to do something about it by running. This was going to help me get positive both physically and mentally.

'Okay, I'll see you in the abattoir,' I said, heading out.

There were 'my' emus in the distance, near the gate to Bedlam. I smiled – that was a good omen. There were sheep coming in too, a long line of them, lambs bleating in the morning sunshine. In so many ways, the Flinders Ranges is one of the most beautiful spots on earth. Was I not lucky to be locked down in all this space? There were whole families holed up in their little houses unable to even go out of the front door. I was free.

I started running through the creek towards the paddock. It was a glorious day, and when you have a flynet on, you can appreciate the full beauty of the trees and mountains, plants and animals, and to top it all off, that all-encompassing blue blue sky. I picked up my pace. How about that. I had energy! I giggled and jogged on. I got to the gate with ease. I breathed in deep and looked around. I could not see the homestead now, but I only felt a pang of jitteriness as I opened the gate to Bedlam paddock. I was not going to be spooked by nothing. I closed the gate sure of the fact that I was getting to that tank no matter what.

After a few paces in, my knees started feeling stiff and I was slowing. No, no, no way am I turning back. What was that? A pale animal passed by a bush, was it being furtive, stalking? It looked like a lion! Oh dear sweet Jesus, why did it look like a lion? For crying out loud, it's a sheep. I was on a frigging sheep station. Lion, imagine what a lion would do to you. Perhaps there's some crazy out there who's got a farm and the lions got out… Maybe the roo shooters are after it and they're aiming right now…

I was running back to the gate like my life depended on it. I couldn't catch my breath and my chest burned like there was some squeezing pressure around it. There was something wrong with my head. Was it agoraphobia? It must be, it was irrational, and it was debilitating. Was I losing my confidence, my fucking mind? How could I go back into the world if I was scared of my own shadow?

No, it wasn't me, it was this place. This outback life of isolation with only me and Steve, Steve and me and no one else. I thought of my family, friends I no longer kept in touch with, thought of all the people who had a life. They had a life. The only life I had was fictional and might not even be read by anyone but Sofia. The people who lived up and down the Flinders Way had a life, all those who lived at

Leigh Creek, Copley, Marree and Lyndhurst had a life. El Cid with his wife and his mistress and his cattle, sheep and oh so many businesses, he had a very rich life. Even through this lockdown, they all had a life around here. I felt like Al Pacino's colonel character in Scent of a Woman, where Charles is trying to stop him from committing suicide and reminds the colonel that he's got a life to live. The colonel roars out, as only Al Pacino can, 'Life! Life! What life? I got no life.'

'I got no life,' I said, reaching the gate of the homestead as I was doubled over, trying to breathe through horrible chest pain and a dry throat. It took a while to feel right again, but when I straightened up, there was Steve. He must have seen me and walked down to see what was the matter.

'You back already?' he said, his face looking cross. He took off his cap and scratched his head. 'You didn't make it to the tank then. What stopped you – too unfit?'

I looked at him and decided to tell the truth. 'I think I've got agoraphobia or some…'

'Acrophobia!' He laughed. A real belly laugh.

I gawped at him, my mouth was still open from being in mid-sentence.

Then I let him have it. 'No, not acrophobia, that's fear of heights, I'm talking agora-phobia.' How I stopped myself from screaming, you dumb piece of shit, I don't know. Well, I do. He would have whacked me one probably. He is no gentleman – that I learned in Saudi.

'Excuses, missus, it's all just excuses. Anyway, good you're back, you can help me with the cold-room. It's a mess in there.' He started walking towards the house.

I stared at his retreating figure. Faaark, what was going on with us, with me, with him? Did he really not care about my feelings one iota? I had the strongest feeling that he wouldn't care if I lived or died.

Because he doesn't care if you live or die, he never has and he never will. He only cares that you feed him, suck his dick, and/or ride him, oh, and be there for him so he can say he has a missus. He won't divorce you because that would be an ignominious failure for him. Remember, he said, 'I won't get divorced again.'

I pushed the thoughts away. They weren't helpful. Quite the opposite. What I had to do was go help in the butcher's room. I hated that room, although I'd only seen it through its mesh windows. It was full of scary tools from the days when farmers were allowed to butcher their own animals, though many still do, licence or no licence.

When I reached Steve, he was looking at rows of meat hooks and chopping blades. They were all rusty, but looked like they could do damage. The floor was full of gecko shit and general insect mess. Steve started investigating things that were strewn around on countertops. He started pushing stuff around aimlessly.

I stopped to look at some instrument of carvery and an indescribable pain shot through my foot. I looked down to see wire sticking out of my running shoe. It had gone through the nylon. I hobbled out of the shed and Steve helped me into the house and into the kitchen where he took off my shoe and sock, and I screamed in pain.

'Fucking mind my ear,' he said, pulling back.

I fought back tears when I saw that the wire had broken off halfway down my toenail. It was lodged in the flesh. Was this day a sick joke on me?

'Will I need a tetanus shot?' I asked, looking at my horror-show big toe.

'I'll need a pin or tweezers. There's not enough wire poking out to get a hold of,' he said, prodding it.

The pain was sending waves of nausea to my head. I started chanting inwardly to keep me from yelling out into his ear again.

'I'll be back,' he said, getting up.

I looked at my toe, thinking of the abattoir. Between the rust, decaying faecal matter, and the cadavers of a billion insects (if bugs can be dead bodies), I was having visions of the fevered night ahead of me where I would become delirious as septicaemia coursed through my veins. It made me want to weep with frustration.

As Steve came back, I said, 'Why does everything around here want to kill you?'

He crouched down and began teasing out the wire. I bit down on my lip and tried not to draw blood – his blood.

'Stop being a drama queen – it's nothing,' he said, scraping around the wire and skin.

I glared at him. 'Ow! Steve, stop, thanks for trying but I'll get it out.'

'Suit yourself,' he said, getting to his feet, handing me the tweezer. 'I'll go back to the cold-room. You stay here if you want.'

I looked out of the window as he passed by and thought, I am so done with you.

## Mustering the Sheep

Steve got a text from Cid telling him that he needed to get the yards ready for a muster. It was not surprising, because the ewes had been lambing in abundance now that the paddocks were green again, adding to the considerable number of grazing sheep already on the lands. Once again, the pastoralists were in business. Cid's working life wasn't curtailed by the Covid lockdowns because he fell into the category of essential worker, as did musterers. Sheep and cattle could be rounded up and processed for sale or tagging or whatever pastoralists did with their livestock. Steve told me about all the work we had to do to get the yards ready for the upcoming muster:

We needed to put out goat gates around the troughs first so as to trap the goats when they came in for a drink. It involved a lot of work because many of the gates in the yards were broken. Cid hadn't done a proper muster in a few years and equipment had fallen into disrepair.

Cid rang Steve to give him instructions regarding the faulty gates and other preparations to ready the paddocks for receiving the mustered sheep. After half an hour or so, Steve told me that Eastwood from TC was going to be doing some welding at Zebra yard because there was a broken gate and panel along the race – that's where the sheep line up to be tagged. Oh, what fun was to be had in the race. Not.

We were to meet Eastwood at his station, TC, because he needed an extra trailer to load equipment. We were running late because Steve had to do a wheel change on the trailer and couldn't find a spare tyre, but Eastwood gave us a friendly 'G'day' when we eventually got there. I liked Eastwood, as I've made clear before. You couldn't not like the guy. He was the hero of romantic novels, though he'd laugh at you if you said so. When he paid you attention, it made you want to lower your eyes under his friendly, handsome gaze. I hoped I wasn't doing that but the frowning side-glance Steve shot me made me think perhaps I was acting a little smitten. How could I not? With his knife belt and dazzling blue eyes, dimples down his cheek like Clint Eastwood and the height to match. I tried calling him Clint in my head, but it didn't work, and since Aussies like surnames as first names, it fitted all the better. Eastwood stuck.

Eastwood's homestead sat in the prettiest little valley, a meadow really, with undulating hills all around. There were houses and sheds and people everywhere. All their children rode horses and razzed around on motorbikes too. The place was buzzing with activity. It was holiday time, and I gather their cousins were staying. What an atmosphere of happy family life we met.

As I was looking around, three brown sheepdogs were jumping up and around us and I delighted in petting them. A boy and girl about eight were in a small paddock on their horses, jumping over not-so-low fences. A girl about ten was mending a bike and two girls were swinging on a long hanging chair dangling from a tree. They were watching the bike-fix intently. A group of what looked like young backpackers were playing cards at a table on the porch of one of the houses. It was the station I had wanted to live on and experience.

A man came out of a shed and waved to Eastwood. He shouted, 'You get that Amirda fence up, son?'

Eastwood gave a thumbs-up.

The guy came over and said to Steve, 'You Cid's new caretaker?' Steve told him that he was, and the guy said, 'See that you do a good job of keeping his dorpers out of my paddocks, eh?'

'Dad, wind ya neck in, eh,' said Eastwood, shaking his head but smiling.

So this was Eastwood's dad and Cid's schoolfriend turned archenemy. Cid and 'Dad' hadn't spoken properly since Cid had introduced dorpers into the merino area twenty years ago. He suspected Dad sent pictures to the Pastoral Board of his dorpers shagging TC merinos. I thought, good on you, Eastwood, for refusing to get involved in any of this feuding-neighbours crap.

'Just so they know, son, just so they know,' said Dad, heading off again towards the girl mending her bike. 'How you doing, Tilly? Got that chain back on yet?' he asked her.

She nodded without looking up from the fiddly work she was doing.

Eastwood said, 'Don't pay no attention to my dad, eh. They old boys like to rattle each other, that's all, eh?' He said 'eh' a lot – it's real outback lingo.

'Where's Bella? I asked.

'She's helping on the film set out in the desert. Think she's teaching Russell Crowe how to ride a horse, eh.'

'Wow, seriously?' I said, feeling the sting of envy again. I was getting battered this day. I smarted a lot when around Eastwood and Bella.

Eastwood then said, 'Or she could be scrubbing out the dunny. Depends, eh?'

Ah, I loved this guy. He looked down at a pretty young girl who'd come over and was now cuddling his knee. She was his youngest daughter. She was three years old and already rode a horse, plus, like her older sisters, anything with wheels. Yet, for all their physical robustness, the girls were gentle like their parents. It was because of this collective charm I called their station Tuesday's Child (cut to TC), because Tuesday's Child is full of grace and everyone in this family was full of grace. Well, perhaps not Dad!

Eastwood put a hand on the girl's braids and said, 'You coming to the scrapyard?'

She nodded. I thought, I bet you never have to watch your dad vomit into a handkerchief day in day out because he's dying of self-induced liver failure. And you'll never have to cry with aching guilt years after his death because you can't bear how he suffered a lonely life you never bothered to inquire after. My dad would have adored this place, if his love for cowboy sagas was anything to go by. Took me ten years to get over his death, and there was a time I really thought I never would. But I did grow out of the grief. I'll never know why he couldn't get his shit together. I hope I'm not too much like him in that regard, and at least I'm trying to work out why I mostly feel unhappy. God, this country, these stations, they're like some collective psychiatrist's couch for me, except it was high time I got off it!

We drove on to TC's junk- or scrapyard, which was almost identical to Cid's. It was full of old cars, gates, all kinds of defunct machines from dishwashers to fridges. There were piles of metal pieces everywhere. Eastwood stopped at one such pile. We got out and I watched his daughter, under Dad's instruction, fill a crate with what, to the untrained eye, looked like bits of useless rusty metal of the kind I had sifted through those first months at Amirda.

When we finally got to Zebra yard, I would see that what looked like a box of shit was a trove of essential components to create locks and replacement hinges for defunct gates. As sparks zapped onto Eastwood's iron mask from the welding gun he was using, I saw he was creating a new paddock out of the old, like Frankenstein creating a human being out of parts of dead bodies. I realised that these so-called junk- or scrapyards that farmers grow are precious resources for recycling, an on-site DIY store in fact. It was their Bunnings in the outback, or B&Q to us Pommies.

That day, we had a barbecue outback fashion in one of the creeks. Eastwood got out a square metal plate with legs that folded down. It looked like nothing but with a few twigs underneath then some bigger ones as the fire took effect, hey presto, within a matter of fifteen minutes glowing embers emerged from the flames and we had a barbecue going. Eastwood threw on chops and sausages from a cool box. We even had cups of tea. Like before, Eastwood put a metal cylinder with the top cut off on the side on some smouldering wood, which boiled in five minutes.

Eastwood asked Steve if he played cricket.

'I do,' was Steve's enthusiastic reply.

Eastwood said he was welcome to play for Copley; they never refused a good man. The first game would be in November, beginning of the season. It was a while off but something to look forward to. For me too – I might get some female company at last if I were still there, and it looked like we might be.

As the day came to a close, beers came out. It seems that every farmer has a cooler full of beer for the end of the day because a day doesn't end until you've washed down the dust in your throat with 'a cold one'. Not that I've ever heard a beer called 'a cold one' in Australia, nor have I ever heard anyone say, 'D'ya want to knock the froth off a couple of cold ones.' Especially out here, where beer is generally 'piss'.

'So you'll be mustering tomorrow, eh?' said Eastwood to Steve. It took Steve by surprise as it did me.

'I don't know,' said Steve. 'Didn't think it was right away.

'I got a muster myself, eh. Think we might be exchanging a few sheep in the next few days.' Then he said, 'Did you meet his missus yet?' He was referring to Cid's wife.

We shook our heads. I asked if she was coming up for the muster.

Eastwood said, 'Yeah, she's a good rider, eh.'

Steve checked his phone on the way back and saw he had a text from Cid. It said that Cid was coming up with some people from his place, and if it was okay with us, they'd stay at the house. They were to help with the muster.

I said, 'The more the merrier.'

Steve was not happy that they would be house guests, but he didn't have a say in the matter, really. No doubt he was reeling at the thought of his sauce and oil bottles getting knocked out of place.

So I was finally going to meet Cid's other half. I wondered whether Cid would take those calls from his manager while 'the missus' was around. Steve and I took a bet on whether he'd use 'mole-cunt' language while his wife was in earshot.

# From Calm to Chaos

The day of the muster arrived, and so did the entire world, it felt like. But here was life, finally. First, came the elusive wife of Cid. She wasn't driving a fancy ute but an enormous, rattling cattle truck. She looked dwarfed by the steering wheel but I figured it was my skewed angle of vision. She pulled up by the hay shed and opened the door. I couldn't believe what I was seeing when a tiny woman climbed down. She had to jump from the last step. My mind went back to that picture of her with the schoolkids – she was standing in the middle and the adults were on the outside. I had assumed she was tall! Her dark hair was in dreadlocks all the way down her back. Her large eyes, far apart, gave off a bit of an Avatar feel.

'How yuz going?' she said without any friendliness in her voice, looking around and stretching, and if I wasn't mistaken, she'd looked me up and down with a hint of aggression. She didn't wait to hear our reply but began walking away towards the main shed.

I don't know why I had expectations of her being full of smiles and ready to hug me. Why had I expected gushing talk of her journey and asking how we were finding life in the outback?

I spied Cid in his trademark big hat. I waved and he walked over to us.

After he'd said g'day, how you going and all that, he said to his wife, 'What took you so long? Thought you'd beat me, getting here.'

She threw up her arms and said, 'Fucking lazy mole-cunt didn't fill up the truck, eh. I was there at five, eh but didn't have the keys for the tank, eh – had to go back to the fucking house. Then had to come all the way back to fill up the fucking wagon myself. Fucking cunt hadn't done shit, eh.' And so it went on.

This was who Cid spoke 'mole-cunt' with? Yes, it had to be. This was the manager and his wife? It was! There was no mistress at all. I gasped at myself, at how I'd jumped to such a fanciful conclusion.

I just had time to tell Steve about El Cid's 'manager' when we noticed, over by the woolshed, there were men, or boys really, unloading motorbikes off a trailer. Then wonder of wonders, the distinct sound of a helicopter caught our attention. Everyone looked up as it got nearer. We were all craning our necks and shielding the sun from our eyes to watch what looked like something from Chitty Chitty Bang Bang flying through the bright blue sky. Seriously, it looked like a racing car from the 1920s with a propeller on top.

'It's a gyro,' said Steve in answer to my 'What the hell is that?'

The pilot didn't have any cover, like the old-style racing cars. He was wearing big old goggles and a leather hat with ear flaps. He looked like a fighter pilot from World War One. He was a flying museum piece.

Cid came over to us, giving Steve and me a warm handshake. He said, nodding at his wife, 'You met my manager then?' He winked at me. The bastard knew!

Steve and I smiled, nodding.

I said, 'Oh yes, she's great…' Those sorts of things. There was now so much confusion around, I wasn't sure what was going on. But I remember Cid saying, 'And she's your manager now, so be on your game.'

I didn't like that, not one bit. I didn't even work there. Well, I certainly didn't get paid for shit! I hoped he was joking. I was already forming my own name for his wife. You might have twigged that I like a Spanish name, hence El Cid. I nicknamed his wife La Señora Mole.

We watched the gyro landing behind the woolshed. It wasn't like a regular helicopter that comes down vertically. It needed the distance of an approach like an aeroplane. When the pilot came to a stop, we were all walking over on mass to greet the Biggles lookalike.

It took a while for the blades to ease off, and it was obvious that the pilot couldn't get out until the propellers came to a complete stop. I was surprised to see only two blades, and they were really long. When they eventually came to rest, they drooped down to the ground.

Behind me, I heard La Señora Mole say to Cid, 'You should have got a real chopper, eh? That thing ain't gonna muster shit.'

Cid growled a few curse words, hard to say who at, as he went to greet the pilot. I was hoping some of the musterers might be from Urdlu but no, they had all come from an agency near Adelaide. They didn't all know each other either.

Cid told Steve to get the ute ready. 'We'll get the yards set up.'

Everyone was suddenly busy. The musterers went back to their bikes. The chopper guy went with them. Steve went off with Cid and I realised I didn't have anywhere to go. The house was no longer mine, the owners were here. What the hell was I supposed to do?

My problem was solved when La Señora Mole shouted over from the shearer's quarters, 'Can you give me a hand here, Loraine?' She was opening up the bedroom doors at the old shearers' quarters. 'They need an airing, eh? And them toilet blocks you might want to give a clean out. If you need me, I'll be at the house.'

Need her! Yes, I needed her, to clean up her own bloody house. Just like that, I'd been turned into an unpaid skivvy and I didn't have the guts to tell her to shove it.

Two rams appeared from under the woolshed (it sits on stilts). They were always together. I envied them at that moment. They could go about without being molested. How I wished at that moment to be a sheep, although that was short-sighted, given what they were about to go through.

In the shearers' quarters, the beds were very dusty and the floors and windows needed cleaning. I hadn't inspected the beds before. Now I saw that the sheets didn't look that fresh. A few minutes later, I saw that it didn't matter because the musterers were coming over with their own swags in their arms. I left them to it and went to inspect the toilets. They were clean. Steve had been in there.

That evening we had a barbecue. Thankfully, there were no plates involved – just a few mighty-white loaves, lots of chops and sausages, and a great big serving bowl of oven chips. Too easy. Two of the agency musterers were unknown to the others. They had turned up that very morning and now found themselves in the northern Flinders, a long way from home. The idea of men turning up to a place for the chance of a job seemed like something out of the Great Depression, where the unemployed show up hoping a truck will take them out to a construction site for a day's pay.

Steve started telling Cid about our day at TC station and how we'd met 'Dad'. Steve, why-oh-why I don't know, mentioned Dad's quip about Cid's dorpers getting into TC paddocks.

El Cid's reply was 'Tell him to keep his fences up.' He then went on about how 'That cunt would send pictures of my rams shagging his merinos to the Pastoralist Board.'

We had heard the story before, but now it was musterers who were hearing it and they would likely gossip.

My eyes got even wider when La Señora Mole began to have her say about Dad, and chipped in with 'He's always stirring the shit, miserable f**king cunt.'

If Eastwood had managed to douse the hostilities between these old rivals, Steve had just rekindled the fire.

# Musterers Who Can't Ride

At five a.m., we met La Señora Mole at the barbecue, where she was frying eggs and bacon under a bug light. I had just seen the kitchen was full of sandwich stuff – loaves, a joint of meat with a carving knife next to it, a cheese block, salad stuff, chutneys. I knew what was coming.

'Morning,' she said. 'After ya breaky roll,' which she duly handed me; it dripped grease all down my hand, 'You couldn't whizz up a few sandwiches for the crew, could ya?'

I told her I could. The yellow hues on her face from the bug light looked like she had jaundice, which she might have done, because I suspected she had Jim Beam in her Coke she was glugging down. Boy, could this jillaroo drink.

Steve, after getting his egg and bacon roll, went to join Cid in the office. He was making sure all the walkie-talkies were charged and tuned to the same channel. The young musterers and gyro guy hadn't showed up yet for breakfast. The lights weren't on either over at the shearers' quarters. La Señora Mole let them have it and roared over to them to get their f**king lazy mole f**king c*nt arses out of bed. The lights soon started coming on!

Cid ran up to the quarters to see what was keeping them and perhaps to stop his Señora from causing a walk off. By five thirty, I was loading up the back-up ute with the food and water supplies I'd hastily put together.

But there was still a bit to go when Cid came over and said, 'There's a case of wine in the car with your name on it, and would you mind doing one of your nice roast dinners tonight?' He knew I would.

I went back inside and got out the ingredients I'd need to make the batter for the Yorkshire puddings. If I was making a roast, I'd make a good one.

Steve came in and said, 'What are you doing?'

I told him I was making a roast that night, and this was batter mix for Yorkshire puddings. It was better for the mix to stand in the fridge as long as possible, I explained.

He said, looking angry, 'You just have to make a simple roast, you don't have to do anything like puddings. Keep it simple.'

'I want to make them!' I said, cracking eggs into a bowl.

He came closer. 'You don't need to show off to everyone.' He picked up the flour and walked off.

I could not believe what I was seeing. 'Put that flour back on the table if you don't want a scene,' I hissed.

He turned back and slammed down the flour, causing a white dust cloud. Then he came close and whispered, right up to my ear, 'You wash his clothes, you make his bed, you pick up his dirty undies off the floor – why don't you go ahead and suck his dick?' With that, he left.

I gasped. If he didn't offer a grovelling apology for that freaky outburst, then I leave with the musterers! And for the record, I never had to pick up Cid's undies, they were always in the basket, but I did make his bed – daily, which Steve shook his head at, saying, 'You don't even make our bed.' True, Steve did that.

I went ahead and finished preparing my batter, putting cling on the bowl before it went in the fridge. I finished packing the rest of the eskies with the day's supplies for lunch, snacks, drinks et cetera. Steve came over and I was on the brink of telling him to fuck off, but thankfully, I didn't.

He apologised, gave me a kiss, and said he hadn't slept well, that's why he was cranky. He starting laughing. 'Don't know where that came from, about sucking Cid's –'

I cut him off there. I didn't want to hear that again, but good, the cold war was over. For now.

As the sun came up, everyone was busy making ready for the muster, 'the boys' were either putting fuel in their bikes or revving them up, and Gyro Man was off to the strip to crank up his copter. Gyro Man was cool – he looked like Shaggy from Scooby Doo, and was just as laid back, at least until he got near electricity cables or had to deal with young musterers who didn't know east from west, or shit from Shinola.

I thought my job, following the muster in the ute, was going to be easy – I just had to stick to the main pathway and keep behind the bikes, never go in front, it would scare the sheep and send them running another way. Wrong – I nearly rolled the ute over the first creek because the bank had been eroded and hadn't been graded. My four-wheel training had consisted of 'Just put your foot on the pedal and go for it.'

But once over the steep creek bank and back onto the main drag, it was smooth motoring up to near Leigh Creek. They would start furthest out where Amirda met the BM and Mount Remote. From there, they'd work their way in, getting the sheep and goats into their designated yards one muster at a time. It all sounded straightforward and I was excited to see them all on their bikes driving sheep forward with the eccentric flying machine circling above, with Gyro the pilot foghorning directions down to the bikers. I had my phone at the ready to capture it all on camera too.

It would be over three hours of driving until I came across any of them. I had plenty of time to plan the dinner I was going to make. Cid and his wife had brought so much produce, and even more meat – so many joints. I would be roasting two, one for dinner and one for sandwiches for tomorrow. I would do a cauliflower cheese, honey-glazed carrots, green beans and roasties. I could do a knock-out onion gravy too from those beef juices. And I'd have wine too! I figured Steve would be on his best behaviour, having got that fit of controlling weirdness out of his system that morning. So I felt I was in for a good day.

Time wore on, and I began to get nervous because I couldn't hear anyone on the two-way radio. I kept looking at the number 8 praying that it was the right channel. I knew it was, but still.

Then voices came over the airwaves: 'Am I the only cunt that can tell a goat from a sheep? Bring the sheep west, not the fucking goats.' It was La Señora Mole.

Then the gyro guy was screaming, 'I told you to keep me away from the fucking power lines.'

Several voices were replying but it was impossible to hear them through wind interference and crackles – it sounded like they had the mouthpiece too far away or something. I did catch La Señora Mole saying something that ended in '…fuckssake.' Then it was Cid who was screaming down the line. I was getting super stressed and I wasn't on a motorbike trying to follow incoherent instructions. Oh, my turn would come.

I looked up and saw gyro guy high in the air hovering above a long power line. I headed for the nearest yards, but I somehow got in front of the muster, and bikes appeared behind me. Cid was on the radio yelling at me to go back.

Then La Señora Mole was yelling at Steve, 'Steve, stay with them, stay with them.' A second later, she was going crazy, shouting, 'Where the fuck are you going, Steve?'

It didn't help any of us, certainly not me, when she was talking about 'Go east, or south-north-west.'

I wanted to yell, 'Stop talking to me in compass. I only know left and right, up and down, ya stupid fucking mole.'

My stress levels soared. I was backing up to God knows where. I could hardly see because of the dust the bikes were stirring up. Sheep were running everywhere and motorbikes were criss-crossing behind me as well as in front. I was scared witless that I would either mow down a few sheep or take out a musterer.

The next thing, I see a musterer going up a steep hill and looking like he's tipping too far back, then, holy crap, his bike is in the air. He rolls out of the way, just avoiding being garrotted by the 400 cc, which bounces on impact. It's the good bike, prized by Cid.

I get on the radio and shout, 'Man down.' I didn't know what else to say.

The musterers were already going to see if the guy was okay. Soon everyone was there and off their bikes. Cid told me to come over and do smoko. As we came together, it was soon apparent that this first collective muster had come undone – hours of work lost. The musterer who came off his bike was called Chuck, and everyone started to have a laugh about how aptly named he was. There were a few laughs at me, too, for my 'man down'. But the mood wasn't right for much banter. Chuck was one of the guys new to the agency and none of the others knew him. It was the third time he'd come off his bike, which thankfully hadn't broken. Cid told him it would be his last time on the bike – he was going to the next yard to wait for everyone.

'Make sure the trough is filled,' was La Señora Mole's instruction to him.

Chuck didn't look too happy, and I prayed he wouldn't lose his temper with LSM (think I'd better initial her name from now on). She would have floored him. As Chuck rode off, I felt sorry for him. Everyone was laughing at him.

When the other musterers had gone to see the gyro guy, LSM laid into Cid. 'Can't believe you hired a bunch of useless cunts…'

'It you hadn't had that fight with Sherrie, I wouldn't have…' Cid shut up, maybe because of the look LSM shot him.

So she had been arguing with Aunty Sherrie, the elder of the Aboriginal community at Urdlu, and that's why Cid hadn't hired the local boys, probably fine stockmen too. It must have been about the horses, because no one showed to help Steve get those horses and for all we knew they were still out there on Amirda. Or maybe it was about the roo shooting and not telling us. Whatever, no surprises that LSM had argued with Aunty Sherrie. LSM looked like she could cause murder in an empty house.

LSM started saying more shit about the musterers and that Cid could have got better. He said that he wouldn't be using that agency again and she exploded saying, 'Bit late in the fucking day for that.'

I wanted to move away, but there was really nowhere to go.

In between eating cake and drinking water, LSM and Cid spat at each other about how the team weren't working together. It was horrible being within earshot as they said over and over how so-and-so was a 'stupid mole' or 'lazy cunt' or 'stupid lazy mole-cunt'. Steve and I exchanged glances. I knew he was thinking the same as me: which type of 'C' were we?

LSM went to talk to the gyro guy and musterers, saying they needed to regroup.

Cid followed, not before telling us what a useless mole-cunt she was, and how she interfered with everything. 'Too many cooks, that's what we've got here.' He would have been better off telling her that.

Steve went to join the powwow. I looked on, wondering how we'd get through three more days of this shit.

## The Hills Are Alive with the Sound of...

When you're out all day in the hot sun, you have to drink a lot. Which means you have to go to the loo a lot. I went twice when no one was around, but blokes just go all the time. If you're looking at someone's back, chances are they're taking a leak. Getting back to The Sound of Music. If Maria went on a muster, she would sing, 'The hills are alive with the sound of pissing', or perhaps it would be 'peeing', her being so wholesome and all. There was toilet roll in the ute and a shovel in the back too. I hoped no one would ask me for either of them.

After smoko, the muster was back on. The gyro guy took to the skies and everyone was off on their bikes, hopefully a little more coordinated than before. Spoke too soon – gyro guy shot off behind a mountain and Cid started shouting over the airways for him to come back.

'Don't go looking for goats. I'll get the goats. Sheep, over here, thank you.' Unusually polite, for Cid.

Seconds later, the gyro was coming back. I wondered why the gyro guy was to be paid in goats. Surely a conflict of interest when you're wanting to get all your sheep into the yards? I'll never get to the bottom of the mustering payment system.

LSM could handle her bike well. She shot up hills to reappear somewhere different with a group of sheep running ahead of her. Gyro guy was radioing down to the guys, instructing them how to back her up. Way to go, LSM, I thought – this was her better side, like her bushfire relief efforts reflected in the picture of her receiving a Thank You placard from the schoolkids. It looked like she was leading the muster now. She'd round up the sheep and the guys would take over from her, and push the herd forwards where they'd be shepherded in one great flock to the yards waiting for them. When the last of the sheep in the area were rounded up, Gyro Man zipped off back to Amirda to refuel.

Cid was impressive to watch too as he emerged with a pack of goats in front of his bike. He swerved this way and that, whipping up dust and making donuts, but not to show off. It was to stop the goats from getting away by encircling them, or giving them that impression. You could see how he'd trick them into thinking they couldn't escape him. Next thing, they were running ahead in exactly the direction he wanted them to go, and would run into the specially devised pen that would hold them. Re Cid's skill at mustering, it was one of those moments when you say, 'You've done that before.'

As I drove alongside the mass exodus of sheep to the yard, the musterers began coming to the car with exhausted lambs on their laps, the ones who couldn't keep up. I had to stop so that they could offload the panting lambs into the front of the ute with me. I soon had a cabin full of bleating lambs. Some started jumping on me, when they perked up a bit, and seemed to want to get out of the window. I had to cuddle one close to stop it from getting under my feet. They were bleating like crazy, I suppose trying to find their mothers. Have to say, I kind of liked it. Baby lambs are like puppies, too cute for the hardest soul not to want to say in baby talk, 'Oh, you are woobly.'

As I got to the yard, there were clouds of choking dust swirling around. The sheep coming into the open gates were coughing hoarsely like they had croup. I saw that the gate to the trough was still closed, so I jumped out of the ute to open it so that the sheep had access to the water. I was careful not to let the lambs out, and I was in agonies not to trap any heads in the door. I ran to the trough gate and undid the chain – it was one that Eastwood had newly welded on.

'They're too hot to drink. Get that fucking gate closed.'

I was in confusion until I realised LSM was shouting at me. I shut the gate and put the chain back on. When I looked at the panting sheep, I could see how water probably wouldn't be a good idea. Might have been nice for someone to have communicated it before. I took a deep breath. Whatever happened, I mustn't sook (cry). The day would soon be over – just had to keep my cool.

I was told to put the lambs in the paddock. When I dropped that last one over the fence, it was clear that they were completely and utterly lost. It was awful to see the little lambs bleating at the legs of ewes who would sniff at them, then walk off, leaving the lamb running to the next ewe. It was wonderful when a ewe came to two of the lambs and they began suckling her. They'd found their mum. But the lamb I'd been cuddling was getting nowhere.

More sheep were coming into the yards and there was a crowd surge. My lamb almost got trampled on. I thought, it must be strong enough to survive, it will find its mother. I stepped away because it kept bleating at me like I might be its mother. Some of the musterers got into the pen with the sheep and they all ran towards where I'd put the lambs. Cid was moving them all into another pen. When the sheep had cleared, two lambs, including mine, lay lifeless and bloodied.

I prayed that the lambs had not got rejected because they stank of me. Don't touch the lambs, or their mothers won't want them – I'd heard this but there was nothing I could do about that when they were being pushed into the ute with me. But then, how could the ewes find their separated lambs from among that chaos? And even if they did, they still risked getting trampled in the stampede. I cursed the muster because surely the distances were too long on such hot days. 'The little things just can't keep up,' I said to no one and started to blub. I couldn't help it.

I felt someone's hand on my shoulders. I looked up to see Cid. His bloodshot eyes were staring at me.

He said, 'Come on, be all right, have to toughen up in the yards.'

I wiped my eyes with a dirty, dusty hand and nodded. I thought my own eyes were probably bloodshot now, thanks to the wind, dust and stress, although it would be nothing to what the riders were experiencing. Cid picked up the lambs and walked to the other end of the yard. He hurled both carcasses into the bushes not far off. I closed my eyes and shook my head. I had to let it go.

When all the sheep and lambs were secured in the pens and Gyro Man was back, everyone was off again to muster on the west side. I was back in the ute following, praying no more lambs would be put in the cabin with me.

Two hours in, things seemed to be going more smoothly – there was hardly any cussing down the airwaves. I was happy because I could see most of the riders in the hills and mountains in front. I caught sight of LSM bombing along on her bike following a creek line, then boom! A kangaroo leapt from God knows where and knocked her clean off the bike. I saw the whole thing and could do nothing to warn her.

When I got to her, she was still on the ground. I began shaking as I knelt down by her, thinking that something worse might have happened if she'd hit her head on a rock. 'LSM,' I said, tapping her on the shoulder. Was she stunned or was she unconscious? There was no blood that I could see.

She started groaning a little, and opened her eyes. 'Fuck me, eh,' she said, beginning to move her legs. In a few minutes, with the help of my arm, she was on her feet, although shaky.

Cid was riding towards us. Before he had his helmet off, his wife was shouting, 'A fucking cunt of a kangaroo…'

I had to turn away for laughing. The vision of her collision with the kangaroo was vivid, and now, her language made it comical.

We decided we might as well stop for lunch and everyone re-grouped. Her bike was put on the ute and she was now a passenger, with me driving. Her side was bruised, but she didn't think anything was broken. I said she should get an X-ray in case she'd fractured a rib.

'Fuck that. You think these lazy cunts will work if I'm fucking…' She started f-ing about, well, just about everything.

To get the manager off verbally abusing her staff (it was too close for comfort), I asked what her family was like. Cid's ancestors were on the walls but what of hers? I was being nosey, plain as. If I'm honest, I was also being a judgemental Pommie snob. She didn't speak like her husband and I suspected she was from a rough background. I wanted to know. Come on, that potty mouth, wouldn't you?

'Did that cunt of a husband tell you I was his housekeeper? That's where that fucking question come from?' she said in answer to my 'Are your family from around here?'

'No! He told me you're the manager, that's it.' My look of surprise and horrified confusion that went with this truism must have told her that Cid hadn't betrayed her.

She sniffed and looked out of the window. She was probably hating me because she'd gone and given away her secret for free. 'Well, I'm telling ya. If you meet his stuck-up cunt of a family, they'll tell you about how I come from nothing.' She turned and looked at me. 'They hate that I can buy and sell the lot of them now. Got million-dollar properties coming out of my arse.' She shook her head and laughed, saying, 'They'd still be shearing fucking maggot taxis and making no money if it weren't for me, eh? Fucking moles.'

'Maggot taxis?' I questioned. I'd got the gist, just wanted to hear more.

'Fucking merinos,' she said and stopped laughing. She picked up the car radio, saying into the mouthpiece, 'Not feeling good, going back.' Without looking at me, she said, 'You can turn around here and take me back to Amirda.'

I told her she'd have to guide me back. She nodded as she put her head back and closed her eyes. Great. Luckily, I did find my way back, as she was snoring, and smelling of liquor!

When we got to the house, she said, 'Get back to them quick, eh,' and slammed the door.

I felt my cheek get hot at her behaviour. How dare she slam the door on me and give me a command like that. I drove off seething, and then I thought, even despite her affair with Jim Beam, the woman just had a nasty fall. Wouldn't I be out of sorts if a kangaroo had thwacked me off my bike into the dirt? Although, if I'm honest, at that moment, I wasn't sorry it had happened to her.

# The Homestead Turns into Downton Abbey – Yes, M'lady

The yard was a hub of crazed activity. The sheep were being loaded into the race, where Cid was going along the line clipping ears, tagging ears and spraying woolly backs with different-coloured spray paints. He was barking orders at Steve, who looked to be having a hard time keeping up with supplying the correct colour can, or the right tag or the right clipping gun. Steve looked all fingers and thumbs as he struggled to give Cid the correct item. Steve's shirt, as well as Cid's, was spattered with red. The bloody pierced ears of the sheep said why. The other musterers were doing different kinds of tagging in another pen. Chuck, the one who had come off his bike, was struggling to hold a feisty ram as another lad put a small band on its nut sack. They were castrating too, obviously. I felt bad again for chuck as he struggled to keep his face away from the kicking ram's horns while Cid yelled over how he was doing it all wrong.

I looked over at the paddock full of goats. Nothing would be done to the goats save for them being loaded onto a truck for the abattoir. Some billies with large horns were head-butting each other, then the winner was humping a female. It was then I noticed that a lot of females were being chased and shagged all over the pen. The more I watched, the more disturbing it got. It looked like the female goats were being raped, and I say that because they were trying to get away, only to get pinned in a corner and then mounted. One would get away and another goat would be on her. It was horrible, like watching some vile misogynistic movie. I suppose I'm anthropomorphising, but still.

Over in the other pens where sheep were waiting to be put through the race, mothers were calling to their missing lambs and the lambs to their mothers. Some had found each other at the pen divides, while others were still going in and around the group looking for each other. I looked out towards the peaceful mountains, but the incessant bleating and Cid's shouting brought me back to the pens. But thankfully, it wasn't too long before Cid called it a day and told me to go back to the house and see if I could help LSM with anything. She was lying on the couch when I got back. On the table near her was a Coke in a stubby cooler and a bottle of Jim Beam.

'Gotta knock myself out, eh? For the pain.' She sat up and drank some Coke, saying, 'You can prep tea now.' She then flopped back, resting her drink on her chest.

'Okay,' I said, feeling like a servant taking instruction from her mistress. It was Downton Abbey – a very skewed Aussie version.

When she didn't say anything else, but had another drink with her eyes closed, I left.

I was near the kitchen when I heard, 'Close the door, will you, hun.'

Now in my role as maid, I walked back and closed the large double door, mouthing, 'Yes, m'lady.'

She was on her phone, saying, 'You fucking won't believe what happened to me today…'

When Cid and Steve came onto the veranda sometime later, I was on my way to get eggs from the coup. Cid told Steve to take a couple of bales of hay up to Bedlam yard. Maybe one lucerne too, for the goats. Steve stood up from taking his boots off. He didn't looked pissed off, though, far from it and acted like this was no trouble. Why could he not do that for me?

Three bales meant three trips in the tractor. Cid explained that putting the bales in their stand meant opening the pen panels. Steve would have to have the tools from the ute for that. Cid asked if I'd help Steve. This was an hour job at least. I felt like it was a case of no rest for the wicked. Yet LSM was lounging on the couch!

When Steve and I finally got back to the house again, they were in full party mode – the table outside was full of drinks, burst packets of Doritos, cigarette butts and dip jars.

LSM still had her Coke, and now it was Bundy rum on the table. She said to Steve, 'You took your time, eh?' as we approached the table.

I saw Steve was in mute mode so I went to say something about how we were all finished and the yard was ready for sheep, but she turned to one of the musterers, and said, laughing, 'No, fuck you, that bike weren't too powerful. I'm not Taz Boy. It was that cunt of a kangaroo knocked me off.'

Everyone started laughing hard, and then people started shouting at the same time.

Gyro Man said, taking a cigarette out of his mouth, 'And when's that cunt gonna learn his right from left?'

I was amazed – all grievances were forgotten. That was just the heat of emotions talking out there. Impressive. But that night, Senora Mole told me that she'd be heading back to Adelaide to see a chiropractor. After coming off the bike, it seemed after all, her joints and back were out of alignment.

Her parting advice to me was 'If things get too much, just fucking drink, eh?'

I took her advice with dire consequences.

In case you're wondering, I didn't bother with my Yorkshire puddings that evening and Steve was happy I served up a basic roast, which no one was that keen on eating anyway – they were all pissed except Cid, who asked for seconds.

## Carrying on Like a Pork Chop

The following days for me were a blur of prepping. After I had done breakfast, there were the eskies to pack for lunches and smokos, plus remembering hot water flasks for tea and coffee. I told everyone they were in charge of getting their own water – even Cid, although he was making a fine mess in the kitchen when he filled up his new-fangled water backpack, splashing water everywhere. I had to add daily mopping of floor to my duties.

I got out of the end-of-day yard work by insisting I go home to prep dinner. I baked cakes, made a giant lasagne, or cooked up a Desperate Dan cowpie. I was only catering for eight but it might as well have been for the five thousand, as Steve pointed out.

I was almost in a frenzy over making enough food but, more importantly, making sure I did everything right. My efforts were getting noticed and my dinners, teas were getting heaps of praise, particularly my Yorkshire puddings, which I served up the day after LSM left. Cid labelled them 'Pommie pies', and wanted them every night no matter what was on the menu. The trick is to use really hot oil or, in this case, smoking lard. This makes the puds rise to the roof and taste heavenly too when made with lots of home-grown eggs and quality beef fat. If they had failed to rise, I believe I might have fainted. I was also liking the wine and having way too much of it, but since everyone was drinking, I didn't rein myself in.

When I sat down to eat, I was so high on adrenalin from obsessively watching the oven, washing up pots and wiping down surfaces, oh, and more floor mopping, I talked instead of ate, and this was usually in the form of telling homegrown jokes, like 'You Aussies can go either way when it comes to politeness and enthusiasm. There are the people who serve you in shops or pubs. They can go from looking through you like you don't exist. Example, you ask for fish and chips and the server goes, "Be ten minutes, that's ten bucks." Then the next place is something like the opposite, where you become the centre of their universe. You order a meal and they'll be like, "Awesome, too easy, no worries, mate. You are so welcome. Just need you to tell me where you guys would you like to sit today, and we will bring it right over." You need a sit-down just to recover from the onslaught of positivity.'

Steve was glaring at me to shut up, but I wouldn't because too many of the musterers were liking my reflections, if I can call them that.

Another night, after I had brought out my giant shepherd's pie, I regaled everyone with my 'funny experiences around Oz' stories. This one was about a dying mining town north of Perth. 'We go to the bar of this one-horse town, and I can't believe I'm looking at suicide prevention leaflets. I thought they were the lunch menus. We got a pint and sat down. A guy starts up a conversation and tells us his wife left him, took the kids, and now he's living alone in the run-down caravan park next door.'

Someone said I was like a stand-up comic.

Boy, did that spur me on. I said, 'During this uplifting tale…' I paused for laughter and got some, but not from Steve who was glowering in my direction. I carried on, '…there's a deafening ruckus at the door, people banging shouting and carrying on. The landlord is over the bar and locking the rabble out, but the banging and shouting goes on. Our friend of the woeful tales says, "Don't worry, it's just some drunks trying to score meth." The music playing sounds like a funeral dirge. All this was making me want to pick up one of those leaflets.'

I got some laughs, but Steve was shaking his head.

On the last night, Steve asked me not 'to carry on like a pork chop'. Pork chop, pork chop – oh, did I have a great anecdote about not carrying on like a pork chop, and the tale involved Steve.

Just to spite him, when there was a lull in the conversation, I took centre stage with this. 'I love Aussie sayings, and one of my favourites is when someone is described as "carrying on like a pork chop". I love that one.'

'Carrying on like a what?' asked Taz Boy.

I said, 'Like a pork chop, meaning someone is behaving inappropriately and making a fool of themselves.'

I heard Steve mumble something to the effect that that's what I was doing, but I ignored him, saying, 'The first time I heard it was when I met Steve's family for the first time.'

I looked at Steve. Oh yes, like I said, bring it on. Surprise, surprise, he wasn't looking amused. I continued as if he was loving my yarn, even touching his elbow as I said, 'We were in a pub and Steve's brother was pissed, as in drunk, and he was eating his hamburger like a maniac and got a slice of tomato on his chin which he didn't notice and just kept on talking. Oh, and now his beer was spilling over as he told some story that involved pointing.' I gave a demonstration of Steve's brother's over-spilling pint with my spare hand.

That got a lot of laughs.

I carried on, 'Steve was getting mad at this scene, and when I tried to get him to lighten up, he said, "I can't watch much more of him carrying on like a pork chop." I burst out laughing because it's a funny thing to say when you're angry. All I could see was a big pork chop dancing around.'

Laughter erupted around the table.

A musterer slapped Steve on the back, saying, 'Yeah, that is a funny expression, bro.'

Gyro Man said, 'I get it, you can't be mad and say "carrying on like a pork chop". Far out. But why a pork chop in the first place?'

I said, 'Apparently it comes from a saying about standing out like a pork chop at a Jewish wedding. Over time, just the pork chop got left.'

Steve was quick to clear away the plates.

When I got to the kitchen, he said, 'When are you ever going to shut up and stop making a fool of yourself?'

I didn't answer but went and got another bottle of wine. When I came back to the kitchen, Steve had gone. I cleared up but didn't go outside again. I was really afraid I was going to fly at Steve and we'd have a stand-up row in front of the guests.

I sat in the kitchen and finished the bottle all by myself. Several people including Cid asked me if I was okay, while getting themselves a drink. Before I knew it, everyone had gone to bed. I had gone and opened another wine and was drunk. But I didn't want to go to bed and get another lecture from Steve.

Eventually, I had to admit defeat and go to bed. When I entered the bedroom, Steve threw something at me. Next thing, I was screaming, really screaming my head off. Steve got out of bed and I ran. I didn't stop running till I got to the shearers' quarters. There was an unoccupied room near the toilet block. I went in and locked the door.

Next, Steve was outside telling me I had to calm down and come back to the homestead. But I yelled at him to piss off, said I hated him and that I was leaving. I don't know what else I said, but I woke everyone up. I was swearing a lot too, no doubt making everyone's mouth drop open with delighted shock.

The next day, I woke up remembering everything, and no way was I going to go back out in that ute, nor make breakfast or lunches or teas. I was done with this unpaid job, this shitty dangerous marriage, and I was done with Oz.

Steve tried to talk to me but I told him to fuck off. I found Cid filling up his bike. I asked him if I could use his car to go to Leigh Creek. I would leave the keys at the post office. He agreed, looking bemused. I was amazed he didn't try to talk me out of it. I took his hand and said I was sorry. I was crying all over the place. I begged him not to tell Steve where I was going. He promised, still looking completely bewildered like he didn't know what was going on.

I waited till they all left in the cars and bikes before going back into the main house. Then I threw together a suitcase, got my computer and left in Cid's big shiny ute. I decided to go the back way, past Camel-foe paddock to avoid being seen by Steve and the musterers. It was hard for me to see as I drove because I couldn't stop crying.

Halfway through the journey, I saw a ute with sheep in the back. Shit, it was Eastwood picking up a group of merinos. I was going to drive right past him, but he stepped towards the car and I had to come to a halt, sending huge dust clouds over him. He came to the window, and I pressed the button to bring the window down. If he glanced at my luggage, I didn't notice, but he couldn't have failed to see my cases thrown on the passenger seat.

'Everything all right?' he asked.

God knows what I looked like. His eyes were searching mine as though for an answer. I told him I was just going to Leigh Creek to get something from the post office. He patted the window frame and looked like he wanted to say something else, but my forced cheerfulness probably stopped him. He moved away so that I could drive on. I wept with embarrassment, envy at his life, the misery of my own. I don't know that I have ever felt so beneath anyone.

When I got to Leigh Creek, the tourism place was just putting out its sign. I could book into the tavern until either a bus could take me to Adelaide or I could hitch a ride there. I parked away from the shops and sat there. The magic eye picture was trying to come into focus – the signal that I wanted something to be revealed to me, what was really going on in my soul, some shit like that. Something inside was screaming that my will (that is, what I want) and actions (that is, what I end up doing) are entirely separate, like I have some congenital disability working against me. The magic eye self-portrait was blurred, but I could see weakness, my own weakness and no one else's in that imaginary painting.

A mother and her children went past the car. She was a young mum, not more than twenty. What responsibility she had, and she looked responsible too – strong of mind. Perhaps that was part of my problem, that I'd never had children. Was I still a child myself, a young girl grown adult? Before long, I knew I wasn't going to walk into that office and book a room at the tavern or a bus ticket to Adelaide. I was going back, back to Steve, back to I knew not what. Actions were overpowering my will – or was my will, what I wanted, not what I thought?

## Gay Rams

I was horrified to discover that the musterers were not leaving that day – they were staying on to help in the yards, but Cid told me they would be seeing to themselves up at the shearers' quarters. I had no more duties.

'You just take it easy, miss,' were his kinds words. He also joked that I was like a homing pigeon and said, 'See, you had to come home.'

I thought about his wife and her drinking – yes, he was probably used to such volatile scenes. Still, I was embarrassed that I had gone off like a Catherine wheel because, and I had to face it, because I got drunk and lost it.

'Thank you for coming back,' said Steve. It wasn't followed up by make-up sex or cuddles or anything that showed he was thankful I'd come back. Nothing had changed, it felt like. We were both sullen and silent.

Steve was up with the alarm as usual but it must have been a struggle because he was tired, probably exhausted. Cid hadn't done a muster in years and the lambs had grown into teenagers (hoggets), and were fat from feeding on the then plentiful green saltbush. Steve was doing backbreaking yard work, having to lift fifty-kilogram hoggets one after the other for Cid to tag, nut, delouse and whatever else he did to the overheating, stressed-out creatures in the pens.

I recall all this to be fair to him while I was wallowing in my mental fatigue. As he got up to face a gruelling day, I slipped back into the unconsciousness of sleep. It was a dubious luxury that my running away had afforded me. I would have been better to stay awake, because my dreams were uncomfortable, awful. I was having the same recurring nightmares of staircases giving way beneath me, of shopping for clothes but not being able to find any that fit me, of losing teeth, of being someplace like a paradise where I'de be happy only to wake up and find the reality of being in hell and unhappy. There were lots of lions and dangerous dogs that I came across and had to pacify so that they wouldn't sink their teeth into me. I've been having dreams like this as long as I can remember, and they are most vivid and terrifying when I'm trying to change my life and go it alone. Are they interfering with the will vs action dilemma?

Cid continued being very nice and told me that I could do as little or as much as I wanted. 'No pressure.'

I prepared meals but didn't eat with them. I wasn't speaking to Steve but then again, in hindsight, I don't believe he was speaking to me.

Then, at last, it was all coming to an end. The last of the sheep were to leave on yet another enormous cattle truck. The biggest truck arrived at night so that he would be ready at sunrise to load the sheep. All these trucks had sleeping cabins behind the seats. I had the paperwork ready that Cid had prepared. I was to go and give the driver a breakfast bun and wait in the yards for Cid and Steve to come over and help him load the truck.

The sheep were bleating loudly in their different pens, all separated according to age, gender, reproductive capacity and so on. They day before, Cid had released all the sheep that were not ready or eligible for sale. They included newborn lambs, some without their mothers. I was appalled to see that some ewes bolted without making sure that their lambs kept up. There were huge wedge-tail eagles sitting in the trees nearby. I knew it would be a miracle if many of those newborn lambs survived that release without the protection of their mothers.

Later, I saw more bones were scattered near the yards. The eagles did get a good share of fresh lambs and kids from the latest muster. Their small carcasses had added to telltale piles of others around the yard. The eagles swoop from the sky and sink their talons into the tight wool, then they fly as high as they can and drop the lamb so that it breaks its neck or legs and can't run away. A brutal cycle of life that you either get used to or get away from. Alas, I had not succeeded in getting away from it.

Before the sun had even come up, the paddock was full of activity. Cid gave the truck guy the go-ahead to start loading. I was still holding the paperwork, which the guy would sign off on once the sheep were loaded. Steve was carrying cattle prods – one for him, one for Cid. There was no gentle poly pipe now. If those sheep didn't move up the ramp, they'd get zapped in the arse and have some nice language yelled down their newly tagged ears.

As soon as I handed the paperwork over, I left and walked back to the homestead. I saw the two rams coming in for a drink; they'd be out of luck, as the troughs were still dry because I hadn't yet turned them back on. These were the rams who liked to shade under the woolshed.

At that moment, Cid came up in the ute with Steve – they were obviously all done. He stopped the car and asked me what I was looking at – I guess I had been stood still for a while.

I wish I'd kept my mouth shut when I said, 'It's those rams, they're still together after the muster. They found each other. Look.' I pointed in their direction.

Cid looked at the rams with narrowed eyes and said, 'They've turned gay, they'll have to be separated.'

I laughed and said, 'You're joking, right?'

His face was serious. 'No joke. Steve, you'll have to separate them. We'll do it now. You get the trailer ready and I'll round one of them up.'

What followed was awful. Cid ran and got on his bike and did his razzing around wizardry on the thing and within what seemed like minutes he was off his bike and had one of the rams in a headlock. The poor animal writhed around trying to break free and made horrendous squeals of distress and protest – the other ram was looking on and seemed to be baaing, 'Let him goooo!' Steve drove the trailer to Cid and they both got the ram in, although it was a struggle.

'Take him up to Camel-foe,' said Cid, and I won't repeat what names he was calling the unruly ram.

'Now?' asked Steve.

'Yeah, might be best. Get the fuckers out of each other's sight.'

It was a depressing end to a depressing week. I dreaded being alone with Steve again, wondering what ways he'd find to punish me for my humiliation of him.

## Chuck Relationships: Is Steve Making Me Crestfallen?

Steve appeared to be okay and didn't mention my meltdown again after he said, 'Sorry you were overloaded. I'll have to be more aware and supportive.'

I thanked him for his consideration, but both of us were not really giving a shit about the other, and I felt that even Steve might be the one to suggest we call it a day. However, for now, we were very much stuck with each other, unlike those poor rams.

My mother's calls weren't helping. Did I have unrealistic expectations of my mother? And why did I keep thinking of that Christmas holiday in Deggendorf? Deggendorf on the Danube. So pretty, trying not to think of Hitler all the time. Christ, I need to stick to the point. That Christmas Eve, so vile. The whole holiday with Steve behaving badly, at his controlling worst, and her telling me at the airport that I had to leave him. Then Steve surprised her with an upgrade to business class. No mention ever again of Steve not being right for me after he gave her the Willy Wonka ticket to a comfy seat and free bubbly. What did that say about her, about us? It's one hell of a head fuck, I'll tell you. But there was so much more. My head throbbed trying to work out what was my neurosis and what was legitimate hurt. God, where was a good shrink when you needed one?

A nice distraction to my internal overload came in the form of a peacock, of all things. A peacock turned up behind the chicken shed and stayed – it had escaped from heaven knew where. It made a home for itself among the bamboo grasses behind the chicken coop. My curiosity towards the peacock was excited more when it began to fly in to the hen house. To accommodate all of them, Steve and I extended the outside area of the coop. When I began checking to see how the peacock was getting on, it was the chicken behaviours that caught my attention more and I noticed their dynamics with one another – the peacock, they seemed to ignore. However, their interest in each other was intense.

Some disturbing behaviour came to light after one of the chickens died. I don't know how it died, but one morning, there it was, stiff as a board, being eaten by ants. Shortly afterwards, two chickens stopped laying eggs too, and ones they did lay often had shells as thin as paper, so much so that they were squishy to the touch. The hens weren't lacking nutrients, there was plenty of good chook feed as well as scraps for them, so it had to be something else.

That's when I noticed one chicken was literally crestfallen. The red crown-like crest on the top of its head was flopping down. When we put scraps out, one hen chased the crestfallen one away and pecked at it viciously if it didn't take the hint to move away from the scraps. It was distressing to see and I shouted at the bully, but it kept happening. I googled what to do about bullying hens and it returned results.

One article said to isolate the bully away from the group but let it see what was going on. Let it stew for a few days, giving it minimal food and drink. Importantly, let it observe the other hens eating and getting on without it. Some observant person had seen this and worked out the psychology going on. The upshot is, show the bully that it is not in fact dominant and essential to the functioning of the group and it will become more humble. Whether the psychology was correct or not, the isolation worked and she didn't bully again. The outsider's crest returned upright and all carried on well. Interesting, no?

Observing the bird behaviour and the resolution to the bullying (though two hens continued not to lay), I wondered if it might apply to me and Steve. I was becoming quieter when faced with conflict and so in a way my 'crest' was fallen too, the crest being my spirit. Were two chickens battling for domination and I had lost? When he began complaining about the slowness of the Internet and throwing his iPad down, I didn't say, 'Oh, grow up.' To do that would cause untold explosions of 'fuck you' retribution. So I would say nothing and wait for it to pass, or remove myself if I could, although to do that, usually ended in 'Hey, where you going?' I don't want to paint a picture of myself as some cringing picked-on victim, I wasn't that. Perhaps I was more like a resentful child, but one who knew not to push their parent too far or else get what for.

'Did you check to see if the chooks laid any more eggs?' asked Steve in an aggressive tone one morning. 'I'd do it myself but I'm busy working. Remember working, can you?'

'What, sorry?' I looked up from my laptop – I had been writing another chase-up email to Sofia.

'Can't you leave your writing for a minute?' Then he yelled, 'And I'm fucking fed up with feeding chooks that don't lay shit.' But he was looking at me, and it was like it was an indirect way of criticising me – for not being cheerful? For whingeing, for having humiliated him at the muster.

'Steve, please, stop shouting. Why are you always getting so mad?'

He made a fist in the air then bit his fist as if trying to overcome some frustration. 'I'm not mad at you, I'm mad at myself.' His last words ended in an exasperated wheeze.

I wanted to say, I thought you were mad at the chucks. Whatever, it didn't matter, he was just mad. Like me, he was in a rut and didn't know how to get out of it.

We were too unhappy, losing perspective, that's what I was reasoning, although I didn't like it when he said, 'Sorry, sorry. Look, why not come out with me today, on the water run?'

I was going to say no, but he said, 'Yes, that's what you're going to do.'

I closed my laptop and said, 'Sure.'

But as I was getting my boots on, I felt nervous. He was looking twitchy and cross. He wasn't saying much either. I got in the ute but wanted to jump right out again. What was the point? Whether I was in the car with him or at the homestead, if he wanted to do something bad, he could do it anywhere. Oh, did I mention that at this point, I was thinking he might want to chop up my dead strangled carcass in the abattoir?

You can imagine my alarm when Steve diverted from our usual water run path and headed towards a densely leafy creek I hadn't been to before. 'Where are we going?' I asked, and felt my heart pound when he said, 'You'll see, it's a surprise.'

Surprise, surprise – what the fuck kind of surprise is there in a dry creek? I got more spooked when he stopped the ute far short of the creek, and said, 'We need to walk from here.' He got out and began walking.

The creek was rocky, great slabs of rock forming tall banks at the sides. Steve slid down, losing his balance as he walked down its banks. As I got closer to the creek, tears stung my eyes. Was he going to push me down there and stove my head in, or perhaps stage my suicide? Was the rope already in place? As I scrambled down into the creek, I picked up a long thin rock and put it in my shorts. If he tried anything, I'd bash him in the eye.

I should share with you that at this point, I'd half been expecting something like this to happen. Thoughts of Steve turning on me had been going through my mind on kind of a loop, as had the idea that murder is rarely planned. Watch any criminal investigation program and they all say the same thing: murder happens in a heated moment. Most of the time, the psycho partner 'just loses it'. That's a quote from a professional criminologist.

Women get their faces stoved in when they unleash the truth onto their controlling boyfriend in a moment when he's exerting too much pressure on her. The physical assault, the evil spontaneous reaction he unleashes on her for her crushing verbal put-down, can result in murder, and that murder is likely to be found out because the ape-shit mess is too much to clean up. Through lack of planning, the murderer leaves a trail of discoverable evidence he can't see. From having a credible alibi to leaving his DNA at the crime scene, to shit just not being right, it's all because he didn't foresee himself battering his woman to death when she told him she was leaving, or told him to get a life.

Where I'm going with this is that before, until this trip to the creek bed, I didn't have any fears that Steve would be violent towards me because he felt like it. No, he would never deliberately harm me, I thought. What I feared was triggering a violent response in him through an outburst of mine. I was scared of what he might do if I launched a tirade of complaints against him, or surprised him with an emotional ambush, and I was becoming very emotional. That is why, however bad my temper got, I didn't want to give him the full force of it or unleash a sarcastic tsunami, because, like I've just said, that's what gets a lot of us women killed. Men snap. Women don't. If a man gets verbally abusive, or worse, physically abusive, the woman will tend to be silent or run. The man in the same situation tends to flip and proceeds to bash the bitch senseless. What I feared now was that Steve had worked all this out and equipped himself in how to commit the perfect murder – that is, in covering his tracks so as to get away with it.

'It's just here,' said Steve, coming over to take my hand as I was struggling to get down from the rocks.

'What, what is it you're showing me?' I asked, feeling for the rock in my shorts.

'It's those ancient cave paintings. Cid finally told me where they are.'

The next minute, I was looking at faded paintings of what looked like emu footprints. Steve, like some historian, talked about how they were created in ochre and charcoal but no one apparently knew if there was a Dreamtime story around their significance. I took the rock out of my pocket and dropped it on the ground, puffing out air with relief.

But what did my paranoid behaviour say about our marriage? Maybe I had watched too many criminal investigation programs where you see men kill wives or girlfriends for the lamest of reasons. I felt like apologising to Steve, but that would have meant the most shameful and hurtful of admissions. I do, however, say sorry now.

That aside, it was a privilege to look at the paintings and think of the Aboriginals who had painted them and feel sad because that life had gone. They might have been the Adnyamathanha people, 'Rock People' (I researched later).

Walking back to the car, Steve told me that he parked out of the way because it was important not to have tracks leading up to the cave where the paintings were. We would also go back another way to make the journey look like we were just driving by the creek. I was impressed that he gave a shit, and again felt the weight of my confused and dark psyche.

The message I received from my mother when I got back didn't help, although I shouldn't be talking about me because she told me she was going to see a specialist because of a chest infection that wasn't clearing up. 'They suspect lung cancer.' Her brother had died from lung cancer.

## Broken Hearts and Mending Relationships

Steve came into the laundry one morning looking for me. He had to go out to get some sheep that had got into a neighbouring paddock. It would doubtless be because roos had created a hole in the fence line – a common occurrence – and consequently Amirda dorpers had got through. Thankfully, the neighbour had rounded them up and Steve just had to go get them. Of course, he also had to find the hole, mend it and check the rest of the line, but I'm getting off the point.

Before he set off, Steve said, 'Remember those rams we separated?'

'How could I forget that?' I said, halting putting the washing in the basket.

'The one left behind is dead.'

'Dead? No! How did he die?'

Steve shrugged. 'Don't know. It's in the creek near the woolshed. Think it might have died of a broken heart.'

I stood upright and Steve came to my side. 'What is it?' I asked as he put his arms around my shoulders.

'Think you've had a bit of a broken heart lately.' A tenderness was back in his voice.

I looked at him as he was kissing my shoulder. 'No broken heart, dear. It's all good.'

He looked me and I frowned – if this was an opportunity to speak my mind, I was wasting it, but as usual, I didn't have anything to the point right then to say about us. We kissed goodbye and he said he'd be back for lunch.

I then got upset because one of the blue-tongue lizards had disappeared. For over a week, there had been just one. I'd learned that they form pairs for life and an anecdote from Cid said that the one left behind can die of loneliness. I didn't think it possible; from a lizard?

But the ram had just died seemingly of a broken heart. What was going on? The lizard left behind wasn't into their food so much. Now I feared the worst.

I carried on taking out washing from the machine, but felt overwhelmed by awful feelings, and the action of taking out washing while feeling so sad was bringing a memory back to me: I was transported back home, my mum still on leave. I am crying in front of my younger brother because of what I'd done to his washing, his footy kits. He loved football, played for several teams, and had many colours or strips. He had given his kitbag to me with an apology – I think he'd been wearing them twice or something so as not to bother me. To my shock when I took out the washing load, it was all shrunk and discoloured – most of the kits were unrecognisable. To my horror, I saw that the temperature was ninety degrees. I had boiled his nylon. I began shaking and crying, but he just said, 'It's okay, sis. It wasn't your fault.'

It would have been at the same time my brother was having a hard time at school and, to my shame, I didn't know about it. He was being taunted by one kid in particular, who was singing at him, 'Where's your mama gone?' News of the family's abandonment by Mum had got out. My normally mild-mannered, gentle little brother had snapped. He launched at the boy in mid-song, yanking him to the ground, I guess in a violent frenzy. A PE teacher came to the boy's rescue. His face was all busted open at the eye, because my brother was repeatedly crashing his face into the kerb, daring the boy to sing the lyrics again. The PE teacher managed to convince the boy not to take the matter further and say it was a 'fair fight'. I will remain ever-grateful to that teacher.

# Months Pass by and I'm Talking to Spiders

Maybe a month later, I found the second blue-tongue lizard dead by one of the trees in the orchard. I hadn't seen it for a week and was wondering where it could be. I was watering a mandarin tree and there it was, looking asleep but a pale weird colour. The smell when I nudged it confirmed it was dead. Who knows, perhaps they were an old couple – the grey nomads of Amirda.

It was hard to believe that over half a year had gone by since I'd sent my book off to the agent, and very little had happened in my life. Sofia still had my book, but the publishers were not biting as yet. Sofia just kept telling me she'd chase it up. She talked about Covid being a strange time and everything was moving slower than usual in the publishing world.

It was June and Amirda was cold, especially at night, horribly cold. The old fire smoked, probably because the chimney was blocked, but, unable to make it right, we coughed a lot and our eyes stung. But there were no dramas between me and Steve. I helped him with the water run and with chores around the house. I had even made a little pathway out of slate that El Cid was really chuffed with. It certainly cut down on the soil footprint across the veranda. The days were usually sunny and passed without incident. I was still a bit podgy, but Steve wasn't bugging me about it – too much. I didn't care much either.

July came and the states were coming out of lockdown. I was reading about a comedy school in Adelaide that had places for any wannabe comedians. I read the ad out loud. 'Learn stand-up comedy from pro comedians.' Comedy, there are schools that teach comedy in Australia, how about that? Was it not something for me to pursue? I loved telling jokes – I made comedy notes all the time. Why shouldn't I have a try at stand-up? If nothing else, it would get me out of the sheep station for a while and give me a diversion while I was wating on Sofia to sell my book. It would be a creative release, certainly a creative experiment that might yield, well, who knew what psychological benefits?

The school was run by one Dj Donte in Adelaide.

Steve called it clown school when I showed him the ad. He laughed and said, 'You, with a PhD, want to tell jokes for a career. Now that is funny.'

'Not as a career, no, but something to strengthen my confidence, give me a release from the mental pressures that get me down.' I stopped talking. He wasn't listening – think I lost him at 'strengthen my confidence'.

He was watching the news, which was giving out SA's latest Covid figures. He said, 'It's still a mess out there. We're in the best place. Why would you want to go to the city now?'

Ignoring his fair point and pretending that he had shown interest in me wanting to learn stand-up, I said, with gushing enthusiasm, 'You won't believe how lucky I got. Donte only does the school in Adelaide a couple of times a year because he lives in Sydney. But now there's an opening because someone dropped out. This is for his class in three weeks. You only need three to five minutes' worth of routine and, honey, I've got an hour's worth already. My problem will be selection, and that's not a bad problem to have. Don't you agree?'

By the end of my little speech, Steve was looking at me in a very puzzled state. I think my reverse psychology had worked because he said, 'Oh, do what you have to do.'

I didn't push him any more. That was enough of the go-ahead I needed. I would book myself on the course when he was out – no use letting him see me do the deed. He might intervene. There were guests coming in three weeks for the Christmas-in-July holidays, as they called them. I wouldn't be needed – they were self-sufficient up at the shearers' quarters. However, if Steve saw that the dates clashed, it would be another reason to say I shouldn't go.

I opened my Samsung Notes and looked at what I'd been writing about the Aussie dialect. I removed myself to the kitchen, telling Steve I'd start the tea. I didn't want him to see me at my comedy.

There was a huntsman spider on the kitchen wall. I looked at him as I opened my notes on 'The Things Aussies Say'. I whispered to the spider, 'Do you find this funny?' and read out the following (Steve was rooms away and couldn't hear).

> Quirky and strange things go on in Aussie pronunciation. Ferry is pronounced 'fairy'. People sound like they live in Pixieland when they talk about taking a fairy to get somewhere.
>
> Debut is dayBOO not daybyou. Why do Aussies pronounce necklace as two separate words: neck-lace? Makes me think of Shakespeare with the frill around his neck. Why are hostels hostels? Aussies do the same with place names. You have Ex-MOUTH not Exmuth. We are not used to thinking of the mouth of the river. Then there's the lounge room. Why not just 'lounge'? And why is aquatic pronounced 'aquOtic'? Where did you get that big 'O' from? Then again, you pronounce the measurement of a 'ton' like the 'o' in the name Ron. Yet it sounds so strange. We say 'a tun of bricks'.

'Could I really develop that into stand-up? What say you, Mr Huntsman, or Ms Huntswoman for that matter?' There's a cross-country bus that could take me to Adelaide. 'What do you say, huntswoman spider, do you think Steve will agree?'

'It's not Steve's call,' I heard the spider say.

I said, 'I think you're right. You know, for a spider, you're pretty intelligent.' I looked at the spider again and said, 'You know, once upon a time, I went to the same school as John Lennon had. Hated it, everyone teased me because I had a woolly-back accent, that's a country accent, and a lisp – they would pin me in a corner and get me to say 'sausages and crisps.' Me, a woolly-back, but out here, on a sheep station, I'm a city girl. Perhaps that is ironic. My point is that when I was very young and a country girl, I was really happy. I was not afraid of open spaces and used to walk around the old castle and bluebell woods all alone. I liked to sit in trees miles from people. How about that? We moved to a city when I was nine, and I was unhappy. I'm unhappy again and I need to fix that. I'll go mad if I just hang around with Steve, who, by the way, has been feeding the chickens with huntsman spiders like you, so watch out. Moths too, and anything else he can catch in his hands. He likes to watch the birds fight over you creatures.'

I noticed Steve in the office, listening to me. He shook his head and headed out.

I picked up my phone, went into my emails and sat down. I had Donte's comedy school application half-done. I quickly finished it and pressed send. 'Okay, there's my application email sent,' I said to the spider, but, like Steve, it had gone.

## Am I Going to Comedy School?

I would not say nothing to Steve until I got a place on the course. No use having arguments for nothing – because for sure they would follow. Let them. All I knew is that I'd be staying in a toasty-warm, swanky hotel room. I wasn't going to slum it. Like I said, the house was freezing now, bloody freezing and I was going to give myself a Christmas-in-July gift of a luxurious break, a week off from icy-cold floors that make your bare feet feel like they were breaking into shards. However, Amirda was due to have a lot of paying guests up at the shearers' quarters. Steve would struggle on his own, having to clean up after them and do all the manual chores, but that couldn't be helped. But they did their own catering and were used to being self-sufficient. In fact, they often came when there was no one at Amirda at all. I would be armed with such facts if Steve played the he-won't-cope card.

I got the reply from Dj Donte as I was heading out of the house to help Steve, who was just returning from sawing logs in the creeks. I'd look at my reply from Donte in private. Steve had gone to collect and chop more firewood for the smoky fire. We'd been going through so much of it. Even without comedy school, I wanted to get away from the choking fireplace. I feared for the health of my lungs.

I put my phone in my shirt pocket. I wore the standard station kit now of wrangler jeans and a stiff-collared shirt, thanks to El Cid's catalogues. I walked up to meet Steve. He was piling up large blocks of tree by the log-cutting machine, which looked like some medieval torture rack. When we put it into use, it behaved like one too. In place of a person's head, you had a large piece of tree trunk, but I couldn't shake off the image of a prisoner kneeling next to the chopping blade. In my head, I was seeing an interrogation of Guy Fawkes or Joan of Arc: 'So, tell me, who were your co-conspirators trying to rouse the rebels against the king?' The head on the chopping block isn't saying anything and they close their eyes, martyrs that they are, as the heavy blade presses on their face, forcing through to split their head in two. Yes, I was getting carried away again.

Mind you, it's not surprising, because the noise of the cutter is horrendous and I couldn't be near it for long because I kept seeing exploding heads. Much of the split wood had giant tree maggots, those Aussie witchetty grubs. Gross to look at, big fat yellow things wriggling around. Steve put them aside for the chickens. He would drop them into the pen later and watch the birds eat the things with gusto, just like the huntsman spiders and moths.

When Steve had got back in the ute to park it, I opened the Comedy School email. I nearly bit my bottom lip off, I was so dreading a knock-back. 'Don't turn me down, don't say you made a mistake and there isn't a spare place…' but then I was reading the line '…just follow the payment steps and you've got yourself a place on the course.' I clicked on the link where you made your payment.

Steve was getting out of the car. Should I discuss it with him before I parted with $400? Before I let myself answer, I had my credit card out and was doing the transaction. I was going, end of. I stared at the circle going around indicating it was waiting for the payment to go through. Done. A minute later, I had the confirmation-of-payment email. I was on my way to Adelaide. I just had to come up with five minutes' worth of comedy to work on. Now all I had to do was to tell Steve I was going to clown school. I'd tell him maybe at the end of the day, or in a few days.

I told him a few hours later. He looked at me with a face I couldn't read. A twitching muscle suggested he was mad.

Then he said, 'You've got a place on the course, or you've applied for the course?'

'I got a place. I had to snap it up before it went. Someone had dropped out.'

'When is it?' He still wasn't smiling.

I felt my palms get sweaty as I said, 'In just over two weeks.'

I won't bother to repeat the conversation that followed. He wasn't happy and said I'd have to get myself there. He was saying some crap about how he wouldn't be able to take me to the bus stop, but I knew I'd bring him around. The best news was, I was going. I wouldn't say any more about it until the day of leaving. Knowing Steve, he'd think I'd forget about it. He could be a bit ostrich-head in the sand about a lot of things. This time, I would take that neck in both hands and yank his head into the blinding sunlight of my life.

# Getting Ready for Clown School

While we waited for the Christmas-in-July guests to arrive, I was practising a comedy routine I'd put together. It was the routine I would practise when I got to comedy school. Okay, it was a possibility – I was unsure about its quality. The problem was, I had no one I could practise on, or take advice from, because Steve was in no mood for comedy, let me tell you.

I read the title, 'Aussie Men and Sexism'. I'd written

If sport is any indicator, Aussie men are no way as sexist as their British counterparts. Take women's football, or cricket or rugby. It's mainstream here. Not the case in the UK. Over there, if you're caught playing any of those 'male' games, you can be burned as a witch.

Pause for laughter.

Seriously, you can hear the disapproval in male commentators. When a male cricketer comes on it's 'Here's Williams now, he's a big strong lad, he's a big six-footer.' But when Williams is a woman, the commentator says, 'She's a big strong lass, she's a big six-footer, but I wouldn't fuck her.' Then he turns to his co-host who's looking shocked and says, 'Well, you wouldn't, would you?'

As soon as I read the lines again, I doubted their ability to get a laugh. That was just a bit shock-jockey, wasn't it? Plus, in these woke times, the audience might not get that I'm criticising sexism and instead see me as sexist. I was too inexperienced to handle this material – I didn't need a comedy school to tell me that. Back to the drawing board.

A thundering noise outside told me that Amirda guests had arrived. I put my phone away and put my game face on. Hello, how are you? Happy to make your acquaintance, that type of look.

I went up to the shearers' quarters to see Steve so we could greet the guests together. There was a convoy of vehicles arriving and the dust they were kicking up blocked out the sky. As they came closer, it was like watching the circus coming into town. The first trailer was a vision of blue and silver, its chrome edgings glinting in the sun. All bikes and quads had their own clamps and strappings, and it was like they were on display. The next vehicle was silver and black. Again, lots of shiny new bikes and quads were parked in their own slots on these custom-made trailers – had to be.

Smaller trailers attached to huge sleek cars began parking around the shearers' quarters. I was seeing lots of private number plates. As people started to get out, I saw it was all men, men and boys. They started to come over and introduce themselves. The boys had that private school attention to being polite – they looked you directly in the eye when they shook your hand, but at the same time, these young guys seemed genuinely pleased to say 'hello'.

The grown-ups were all oozing money, money and looks and salon-ready hair. These were slick city boys with flash toys. As they began mingling with each other after their long journeys, one guy started pulling open a cupboard on his trailer. It was a barista-style coffee machine. The machine was surrounded by drawers. Inside the drawers were biscuits, chocolates, creams, sugars, you name it. He offered Steve and me a cup. He was clearly Italiano – not his accent, but for sure his parents were from 'the old country'. He had jet-black hair that fell in long curls above big brown eyes. When he smiled, his straight teeth looked super white against his dark lips. I was trying not to swoon but giggled way too much as I took my coffee. I knew Steve would be rolling his eyes.

These were the SA millionaires who owned big-name wineries in Clare and flash department stores in Adelaide. Drinking good coffee, Steve and I watched in amazement as they unpacked. It seemed they thought no luxury too indulgent. Boxes and boxes of every kind of food, every kind of drinks, were being unloaded from car boots and the trailers. They even had portable fridges. We looked on in awe as large white pillows and big heavy swags went into the humble rooms. The elaborate sleeping swags looked like they'd keep you warm at the North Pole, they were so bulky and fluffy. Some even had electric blankets in them.

Steve and I left them to settle themselves in.

Shortly after, dark flames in the distance showed they'd lit the fire pit. I wondered what their wives were doing. Doubtless having their own half-term holiday with their daughters. These people were so set in life, so happy, so bloody rich, but nice with it. And here were fathers who didn't go off on indulgent golf retreats but holidayed with their sons every chance they got, if the investment into those custom-built vehicles was any indication. I thought of the happy faces around that campfire. Steve was not looking happy this night – I knew he was resenting the fact that I was going to Adelaide. Yet I was going!

# All Booked for Adelaide

The next morning, I booked myself into the Hilton Express for five days and I'd also booked a seat on the Flinders Hopper, or whatever they called that bus. I prayed there would be no level four lockdown crap or any other restrictive evil.

I went to look for Steve to ask if he wanted a hand. He was doing some weeding around the wool shed. He asked me to pull up some bushes in one corner, which I began to do. As I was trying to dig out the root of a large bush with a shovel, part of it landed on my shirt. At least I thought it was, until it started to walk along my sleeve. It was a silvery green stick insect. I had flicked it off in shock but was glad to see I hadn't killed it. I whipped out my phone and took some pictures of Sticky the stick insect. One for my socials (that never got much attention).

In the distance, there were signs of activity among the biker gang. Sons and dads in colourful leathers were razzing up their bikes and forming a line-up in readiness for the off. There were over twenty of them. Soon they were speeding off for a morning of motocross and dust creation. Did they draw straws as to who went up front? I pitied the poor buggers following, copping those relentless clouds of dirt.

When the drama of Sticky and our guests was over, I looked at Steve. 'I've got something to tell you and I don't want you to get mad.'

'Go on,' he said and I felt like I was a little girl trying to pluck up courage to tell her mum that I'd broken her favourite vase. But Steve's unreasonable stance struck me as wholly unfair. As an adult, I shouldn't have to feel like a bloody child.

'Donte's comedy school is in six days…'

He threw his hands high in the air and said, shaking his head, 'It's all good, sweetheart, it's all good. You go to clown school and you pay for it and you get yourself there.' Then he walked off.

He was just letting off steam, I told myself. All the same, I was sooooo glad we had twenty guests.

We hardly spoke for the next two days. I amused myself with posting Sticky on Twitter and got over-excited when a few people commented. Over the next couple of days, I posted more pics of emus, bounding kangaroos, a ewe trying to wake up her sleeping lamb as Steve and I pulled up in the ute. I wasn't getting much reaction, but any response made me squeal with delight. There's probably a word in Japanese describing the action of obsessively looking back at your posts only to find there's been little or no response. The way your gleeful anticipation turns to crushing disappointment. I have these sorts of niggling moments constantly with social media, like the way I follow everyone and no one follows me. Oh, maybe there's a word in English for it already – pathetic!

Our guests were a good distraction. Steve's silence wasn't bothering me too much. If anything, it was reassuring. That he was pissed off about my leaving meant I was leaving.

On their third day, Mr Department Store guy (he owned the equivalent of Harrods in Adelaide) asked Steve and me to go up for a Christmas-in-July drink. Here was a welcome change for us both. Steve and I had eyes very wide open when we saw what an Aladdin's cave of treats they had turned the shearers' kitchen into. It was a grotto of expensive foods and booze. With one cabinet, they had created a cocktail bar.

'What would you like to drink?' asked Mr Department Store guy, who seemed to be the head honcho.

'I can't help but notice the single malt whisky sitting there, so I'll have one of those if I may,' I said while Steve was taking a beer from Italiano.

The head honcho said, 'I'll let you pour. We always do self-pour so that we don't force on people more than they want.'

I felt like saying, then you must be extremely civilised in your set. Do that in mine and you'd be lucky to get your bottle back. Instead,

I said, 'Quite right, nicely put,' and poured myself a triple hoping no one was paying attention. I chucked in some ice quickly before turning round.

'What's that accent? You a Pommie?' asked one of the men.

'Yeah, you know England?'

'I support Liverpool in the soccer, and I love the Beatles,' said Italiano.

'I'm from Liverpool,' I said. 'And I went to the same school as John Lennon.'

'No way,' said someone else, and I was suddenly the centre of attention.

Steve was getting his fair share too. He was being asked how he was getting on in the job and looked happy to tell them. It was good to see a smile on his face and even better that he wasn't paying any attention to me.

'You don't sound like a Scouser,' said Italiano to me. So he knew an accent.

'No, I'm from…'

'But I love the Scouse accent…'

Italiano kept waxing lyrical about Liverpool, but I wasn't listening. I was too stunned. He loved the Scouse accent! How about that? He didn't get that when you have a thick Scouse accent, for some class-biased English people you might as well have 'I'm poor and unemployed' tattooed on your forehead. Gorgeous Señor Italiano owned and ran a prestigious vineyard and distributed wine around the world, but there was no fog of prejudice blinding his eyes, no seeing people as lesser than himself because they didn't have the same privileged background.

More questions were getting fired at me about being a Pommie, and I got to thinking more about a comedy angle for my initial routine in Adelaide. Here I was, a Pommie in Australia, and also from Liverpool, and it was of interest. Plus, they didn't understand why I wouldn't want to talk with a Souse accent. It was the seed of a funny skit.

We soon exhausted the Pommie topic and our little party broke up when the kids asked us to play a few games of darts with them. We played round-the-clock and ate lots of their expensive deli snacks. I once again respected the head honcho's self-pour decorum and got merry on his sublimely delicious vintage whisky, which they were all too polite to notice.

Next day, while busted bike tyres were being replaced (these rich boys didn't do repairs), I went down into the creek to practise my comedy. Steve would be kept busy 'helping' with tyre changes – that is, doing it for them. Perhaps last night's attention might have been to butter Steve up to help with all the punctures, but hey, let's not be cynical. I loved them for keeping Steve busy. Or do I mean distracted?

I wanted to impress Donte and my fellow comics. We were going to perform our final routine at the Laughter Lounge, it had been confirmed. That's a real comedy club. I was going to have my five minutes of fame as a stand-up comedian. Okay, the punters would be friends and relatives of us novice comedians, but still, real comics were going to be there too. Actually, I wouldn't have anyone there, but boo-hoo-hoo, it didn't matter. I just hoped they didn't think me too sad.

Okay, so, thinking of my end performance (had to think ahead), I had spent the morning working on a fresh comedy routine, 'a new beginning if you will' – like the Americans say. Here goes.

> You might tell from my accent that I'm a Pommie. In England people judge you by your accent. I'm from Liverpool and used to have an accent that said I lived in a council house and grew weed in my attic...

I thought, if I do a thick Scouse accent for the ending of the that joke, it will make it punchier. There was more but I'll leave it there.

When Steve came in for smoko, he went straight to the sitting room and switched on the TV. 'You might want to see this,' he said.

It was South Australia's Premier Marshall giving a press conference. Across the screen it said, 'Level 4 restrictions introduced to SA.'

'The state is going into full lockdown,' said Steve, adding, 'All public gatherings are banned. Pubs and clubs to close again. All because a traveller from overseas has tested positive.'

'How long is the lockdown for?' I asked.

'Seven days.'

My comedy course would be cancelled. Sure enough, within half an hour there was an email from Donte saying '…cancelled for now but hope to be back on in the near future'. No refunds would be given because the course had not been cancelled, only postponed. I was so deflated. Donte was still in Sydney. The quarantine rules were too complicated, he wouldn't be coming to Adelaide. I went to the bedroom feeling like I didn't care if I never came back out. Steve had followed me, but thankfully didn't come into the bedroom. For once, he was giving me my space.

# The Bates Motel: I Get to Meet Norman

El Cid had come to stay, and before sun was up, the three of us were driving to the BM along the main road. I was now over my sulk about not being able to go to Adelaide. I would get there in the end – that's what was keeping me going. Cid was doing a great job of missing the kamikaze roos who were jumping in our path with disturbing regularity like it was the roadkill Olympics. We were all in the work ute. It reminded me of the first time I explored Amirda squashed up next to El Cid as he drove. Steve again had his body pressed up against the passenger door and, since he couldn't wear his seatbelt and El Cid was doing about 150 kilometres an hour, he was probably praying, like me, that a roo wouldn't cause us to crash, whereupon we'd join the poor creature as roadkill. Or Cid might swerve, the door fly open and the roo bound off, while Steve and I cracked our heads on the bitumen.

Some hours later, we turned off the bitumen and were on Bates Motel land. The entrance to the homestead was a giant wagon wheel with the homestead name in the middle of the spokes. I was glad when we drove over a cattle grid because there was an enormous black bull chomping on grass at the base of the cartwheel. It certainly wasn't the bull that had scared me over at Mount Remote – that was a Hereford, they're brown with white head and chest. The cattle roaming around were jet-black all over, Cid's Black Angus cows. He had rented Norman's south paddocks for grazing his cattle and now they were to be mustered for sale.

'Looking nice and fat, girls,' said El Cid with a grin taking over his face as we drove further into the property.

'These all your cows, Cid?' asked Steve.

'Yeah, these are the beauties we'll be rounding up today.' He suddenly drove faster as if he couldn't wait to get started.

We stopped in front of a house that was overrun with vegetation and trees. Even the windows were hidden behind the tangled, messy plant life. Half of it looked dead. Its door was opened by a tall man who was as scruffy as the vegetation blocking out the sunlight to his house.

'Come in,' he said.

When Cid went in without taking off his boots, I hesitated. Steve too, and said, 'Don't we need to take off our boots?'

Norman said, 'Not unless they're muddy.'

On entering the house, it was obvious why Cid hadn't bothered with shoes-off etiquette – the ground outside looked tidier. The place was a mess. There were dirty plates and cups everywhere. Stacks of newspapers lined the walls like they were acting as flood sandbags. Tatty old shoes and clothes cluttered the chairs and floors.

'Take a seat,' said Norman.

We all remained standing. I noticed a stuffed Scottish terrier on the mantelpiece.

'That was my dog Jocky,' said Norman.

Looked like the moths had got to his dead pet. Jocky's black fur was patchy.

'You all want a cup of tea?' he asked, adding, 'Before the games begin.'

'We'll crack on, hey, Norman,' said Cid, making wide eyes at me.

I turned away, praying I wouldn't laugh. I saw a side room. There wasn't much in it but a desk with an old-style computer on it and a little chair under the desk. There was a blue light on a box next to it. He had internet, I knew, because Cid said he spent all of his spare time on that computer doing research into God knows what. If you ever wanted to know what someone who surfed the dark web looked like, it had to be Norman. He hadn't changed his clothes in a decade, not even to bathe by the looks. His face was dark from smudged earth, and he kind of smelled like a cheese and onion sandwich that had been left to sweat in clingwrap. Seriously, talk about being on the nose. I dreaded him offering to shakes hands. You just knew his palm would be sticky.

'I'll just tell Mother where I'll be for the next few hours,' he said, going into a room with a curtain for a door.

That is why Steve and I nicknamed him Norman: he lived alone with his mother and was into taxidermy. The set-up was too close to the Bates Motel from Psycho for me not to make the association. They even had paying guests as it was a station-stay, though probably not for long once they saw the filth. Or he killed them off and his mother covered up for him! Jeez, I only just thought of that. Sorry, I shouldn't be so mean. Norman was actually a really nice guy, if a tad freaking eccentric.

Thankfully, we didn't have to hang around the BM for long because the roar of engines outside told us that other musterers had arrived. I couldn't get out quick enough – the house was stifling and pongy. Steve and Cid too were in a hurry. They nearly trampled my heels in their bid for freedom and air.

Steve went to choose a bike from Norman's collection while Cid went to get his motor off the back of the ute. I was to follow them in the ute. They would stop and have smoko in a few hours.

Then began a very long day for me. Norman gave me a map showing where the yards were that I was to go to. It took over half an hour to drive there. One of the yards was full of cattle. Norman had kindly rounded them up for Cid by himself the day before. There were cows outside too, and that meant I wouldn't be able to get out of the car. I pulled up and turned the engine off. All the cattle were staring at me. I waved and some mooed at me.

I got a fright when I saw a huge bull looking my way. I wound the window up a little. They way bulls look at you, it's really unnerving, like they want to charge, which, by the way, they often do. Thankfully, the bulls lost interest and walked off. I got out my phone – I had hours and hours ahead of me and nothing to do, except, I had a lot to do, to practise my stand-up routine.

## I Want a Life as Full as Cid's Wallet

I had three days of driving around, mostly practising stand-up to cows mooing in the yards. It was one of the better weeks I'd had thus far in the Flinders. I was getting pretty confident in my delivery.

On the last day, we drove up to another set of yards at daybreak. The place was alive with activity. Two huge cattle trucks were there to pick up Cid's cows and bulls, and men were busy getting the vehicles ready for receiving the cattle.

The noise from the cattle was deafening – like with sheep, calves had been separated from their mothers and both were crying out to each other from their different yards, letting out clouds of breath into the cold morning air. I couldn't help but wonder how much greenhouse-gaseous emissions in the form of methane and carbon dioxide these beasts were burping out as part of their digestion process.

We piled out of the ute and followed Cid to the yards, where Norman was already moving cattle from one place to another. A lot of cows were shoving each other about and I saw it was because they were trying to get a drink. To look at what cattle do to troughs made me glad all over for Steve that he didn't have to deal with the maintenance of the troughs. Seriously, it's a miracle there's any trough left the way the cattle head-butt any moveable part. Floats are always breaking clean off. The muddy mess they create around the trough as the water is slopped out and trampled in is incredible. Sheep are like dainty Victorian ladies taking afternoon tea in comparison to cattle.

That wasn't the only mess they were making. Cows wee a lot too. Up the tail goes and a great torrent of the water comes out. They do the same while waiting to be loaded on to the truck. Once they are in the race on their way into the trucks, it is a sight to behold. Some cows try to climb over a cow in front that is refusing to budge, especially if it's a smaller cow, and then it gets crapped on by the bigger one. Great big dollops of poop splat on the smaller cow's head. If it's lucky, the heifer will piss it off for them after.

All the time there is mooing and what sounds like the braying of donkeys among the clanking of metal shutters as the cattle are moved from slot to slot, where they are tagged before being loaded on the truck or moved to another holding pen. There is a lot more pooing and weeing going on in the truck too and their hooves slip and slide around until they are packed in so that they can't move. I hated the clattering sounds of cows trying to regain their footing on a metal floor full of piss and poo.

The noise and chaos of the yards reached new levels when the electric cattle prod was used more and more to get the cows moving up onto the top deck of the truck. Then there was a lot of shouting coming from the truck. A guy hanging off the side yelled that a dividing door was jammed and he couldn't budge it. It meant that they couldn't section off the cattle. All cattle now had to stop moving into the truck and were banked up in the race. It was a case of 'If you're queasy, look away now.'

Before things got really nasty in the queue to board, someone had to get in and sort it. Cid declared he was out because he was too big to get into the small space in the truck. One of the young musterers got in among the shit, piss and jittery back legs of the cattle to wriggle the stubborn panel free.

I was surprised when it got to lunchtime. I thought it was still morning, such was the distraction of the tagging and loading. I handed out the sarnies I'd made for everyone. I was surprised to see that no one attempted to wipe or wash their hands and had to hide my surprise when I saw how many brown fingerprints were being made in the mighty-white bread. Perhaps the dung gave a certain piquancy to the flavour, an outback yard relish, who knew? When one kid licked his thumbs clean, I had to take it as certain! Have to say, he was a rosy-cheeked fellow of blooming health, so perhaps he knew a thing or two I didn't about outback hygiene.

When the trucks were loaded and on their way, Cid got his wallet out to pay the musterers who would now leave too. Cid's wallet was so fat with fifty-dollar bills that it looked like a swag mattress rolled up. I couldn't stop thinking about that fat swag-wallet on our journey back. Cid's life was as full as that wallet. It seemed to be a niggling metaphor for the emptiness and poverty of my own life.

## Merino Sheep Are Woolly As…

'We've got guests coming to stay at the shearers' quarters today?' I repeated, thinking Steve must have got the wrong end of the stick. 'Are you sure Cid isn't telling you that they've cancelled? Everyone's in full lockdown.'

Steve shook his head, still looking at his phone. 'He says there's a group of them coming. They'll be here for five days. They're probably farmers so got permits to travel. Wish they weren't coming. The pump is playing up and I can't get water to the showers.'

'I'll air out the rooms then,' I said. 'They're bringing their swags, I take it, like the others?'

'Should be, although the beds all have fresh clean linen on now.'

So Steve had started doing the laundry. It was, no doubt, another mark against me.

The expected convoy of cars with trailers carrying strapped-down motorbikes arrived late afternoon. Steve and I walked over to greet them. Couples and single guys got out of their cars and gave the Covid wave, respecting social distancing.

'You didn't have any troubles getting here then?' I asked, after we'd finished with the intros.

A guy from the first car, called Frenton, leaned into his car and took out what looked like a large vase.

'Is that an urn?' asked Steve.

It was then I remembered Cid talking about having friends who were in the funeral business, and were bikers – all the people who stayed at the shearers' quarters were friends of some kind.

'It is an urn,' he said, holding the thing up a little. 'We're on essential work taking this deceased person to his resting place. He wanted his ashes spread on Lake Torrens.'

'You're kidding,' I said.

His wife Renata stepped in. 'We're taking a detour coming here but it's not against the law. We're all legit.'

They both looked at their friends for confirmation and everyone gave a thumbs-up.

It turned out they were all connected to the funeral business and were involved in the Lake Torrens ceremony. I think it was probably just as well that they didn't get pulled over – don't think they'd have made it to Amirda, but boy, was I glad they did. Like those guys from Adelaide, they were a welcome respite from the loneliness. With these guys, you didn't have to stress and be at their beck and call. These wonderful people only beckoned you to come drink their wine and have a nibble on some nice canapé.

Steve was not as glad of their company as I was, and when one of the pallbearers (clearly not there for work but a holiday), came over to the house to ask if Steve and I wanted to have a beer with them, whereas I couldn't get my boots on fast enough, Steve was slow to move.

When the guy had gone, Steve shot me a weary look and said, 'Hungry for company, aren't you?'

'Hungry? I'm ravenous,' I said, adding, 'And if they ask us to join them every single night, I'll be there.' Oh yeah, bring it on. I was treading dangerous ground, but I didn't care.

Steve did come with me for drinks with the undertakers, but he said, 'And no talking about how lockdown isn't good for their business, hey?'

Trust Steve to mix up the joke. I was talking about how Covid was good for the funeral business. Either way, they were the friendliest people you could meet and they liked a joke – clearly, bringing a dead guy to the party!

As usual, everyone was sat around the fire pit in lively spirits, all competing to tell stories. There was music too; someone had set up a big speaker with pulsating lights.

Whether it was the music, or Steve's censorship I was rebelling against, I said, 'All this Covid is good for business then?'

It got wry smiles. I could feel the breeze from Steve's shaking of his head but he could go hang himself, because I was just getting started.

As soon as I'd finished my beer, Renata offered me a gin and tonic. We had brought beers but I wasn't about to turn down a G&T with ice and lime. Then came questions for me.

'What do you think of Aussies?' This was asked as Renata handed me a second G&T. I liked this lady.

'I love some of your sayings. "He's as flash as a rat with a gold tooth" for a show-off, that's a good one,' I replied.

'Yeah, it is,' everyone agreed.

'Cid has some good sayings, eh?' said Biker-jacket, stroking his beard. 'When I overfed him one time over here, and tried to give him another burger or whatever, he said, "Nah, I'm full as a fat lady's sock."'

Everyone laughed, then someone else said, 'Remember when Cid told the story of a merino sheep that had gone missing – it was back in the day when he was a boy. That merino went missing for four years and then it turned up again. He said all dreamy, you know, like he was picturing that sheep again, he goes, "It was woolly as…"'

I couldn't speak for a few seconds because I had too much to say. I did get it out eventually and said, 'That is one of the few examples of not having to finish a simile. There, I love that story.'

People looked at me, frowning.

'No, listen, you Aussies never finish a simile. It's always, "I'm tired as…" but you rarely say what you're as tired as. Why not just say, "I'm tired"?'

There were a few nods as people thought about it.

'But with Cid's super woolly merino, there's no comparison to anything but…'

'A sheep that's been unshorn for five years,' said Renata.

More beers flowed, more G&Ts were drunk. Steve relaxed and we all tired the stars above us with our revelry. I found out that they occasionally stayed at TC and knew Eastwood and Bella.

I said, 'What a lovely family. Don't think there's anything they can't do.'

'And Eastwood, he's handsome as, eh?' said another very macho-looking biker.

I didn't know whether to laugh because he'd just provided another example of an incomplete simile or for the way he was talking about Eastwood. This guy was with his girlfriend. I'd seen them canoodling outside their room.

Perhaps seeing my confusion, his girlfriend said to me, 'Oh, he fancies Eastwood all right and says that man could turn him gay.'

To my surprise, the macho boyfriend nodded, saying, 'Ah, he's like knights and legends.'

That set me off laughing till I couldn't get my breath. Perhaps it was the gin, I don't know, but I was getting kind of hysterical. I was saying, 'But you can't fancy Eastwood, you're a bloke, a straight bloke.'

To that, he just held up his beer and shrugged.

Steve had to help me home and nicknamed me the Joke Monster.

I went to bed yelling, 'I love Aussies!'

The next day, while nursing a hangover and thinking about Steve's dislike of my joke-telling, I saw four wedge-tail eagles bring down a kangaroo and eat its eyes out while it was fighting them off – to this day, I still can't believe what I saw, but there it was. I was sitting at the end of a pipe waiting for a blockage to come out. Steve was over a hill at the other end of the pipe. He had the water pump machine at his end. We were unblocking a pipe stuffed with shale.

I had been sitting in a dip for ages because Steve couldn't get the machine to start. That is probably why the kangaroo hadn't seen me and was running straight for me with the eagles chasing it. I saw its eye come right out as the eagle's talon ripped through the socket. The cord the eye was hanging by haunts me as I write about it. But it happened, and it interrupted my thoughts about Steve's resentment of me having fun. I was starting to wonder, does Steve just not like it when I have fun away from him?

A burst of water from the pipe hit me. The next thing, I was winded by a block of shale shooting into my chest. It landed on the ground and looked like a poop, a big white turd. I looked around for the kangaroo but it was gone – however, the eagles signalled where it was headed. I can't look at eagles now without hating them a little. After that, it was hard to hear about eagle sanctuaries and eagle rescues. I understood the farmers' point of view. Not that farmers care for roos; they hate them because they make holes in their fences for the sheep to get through, but the eagle is a predator on baby lambs and goats and it's horrible to see those eagles hanging around yards after a muster, eyeing up which kid to swoop on.

We were late getting back to the house that day and thankfully there was some big footy match on TV that everyone wanted to watch. Steve and I didn't speak much. We had been married seven years. You hear of the seven-year itch. Did we both have eczema?

# Up a Gum Tree

The expression 'like a possum up a gum tree' comes from possums running up into gum trees to escape dogs. The possum might be up there scared, or up there resting and happy that the hounds can't reach it. I like to think 'up a gum tree' means you're in a good place. I was literally up a gum tree, practising my stand-up on the dorpers below. Gums are all shapes and sizes. I found one I could easily climb up, thanks to a fallen tree next to it. It was my stage.

I was up a gum tree because I'd had yet another email from Donte, saying that he was planning on coming to Adelaide in a few weeks but he'd hold off on booking his flight – however, he was determined that we'd have our school. Borders were back open and lockdowns lifted, and I needed to build my confidence if I was to deliver to an audience.

In the gum tree, I found that I wasn't practising what I'd written down about the Aussie dialect and accents in general. I was talking about marriage.

> 'The routine of marriage conversation is getting me down. I can't stand it. My fella sits on his coach. I sit on mine. I'm trying to read, he's watching TV and he says something like, 'He's worth a few bob.'
> In reply, I give a 'Hmmm' and nod, hoping he'll shut the fuck up and move on.
> That isn't enough and he says, 'I said, he's worth a few bob.'
> I know he's pointing at the TV screen now. I have to look up. I see he's talking about some presenter who owns a footy club. I don't know the guy, but I have to agree that he's probably quite rich. I mean, give me a break, what does it shitting matter?

Marriage – neither Steve nor I wanted to get married to each other on the day we did. Before the day, I tried to break off the engagement, but he wouldn't hear of it. And yet he was not happy that morning we went to the consulate in Saudi. I sobbed through the vows, great shuddering sobs. Steve's face was stern. I loved Steve in the bedroom, when we had a drink together and he did funny dances that made me howl with laughter, but among people, with friends, out and about, he could make me hate him.

The things he says to me now. 'Remember when you were young and beautiful?' He can see it makes me squirm. Does he enjoy making me squirm? How long have I been biding my time until I can leave? I don't argue with him any more, but then I forget I was ever angry, and we have long periods of marital accord. Yet he only loves the passive, docile me. When I'm behaving myself, only then he gets funny and he's cute and I make love to him, not just because it makes him easier to be around, but because I like him again. Have I developed some sort of Stockholm syndrome with a captor? The tension on my back is so strong that it's giving me a hump. Steve says I look like a Brahman bull. Fuck!

I got down from the gum tree after nearly bursting my own eardrums with the scream of frustration I let out. I wasn't even aware that these things were bugging me in our marriage – not fully. The sheep cleared off as I was screaming, then I skulked back into the house. But I got scared that the day was getting dark and Steve wasn't home. It's not a good feeling to want someone home and not want them home at the same time.

# I Finally Make it to the Adelaide Hills

Donte had booked his airplane ticket. He would be in Adelaide on Saturday. Class would start Sunday evening and our stand up at the Laughter Lounge was Thursday. What day was it? I didn't even know. I looked at my phone. It was Friday. I had already missed the bus. It left Friday mornings. Tomorrow! The only bus on Friday was from Port Augusta. Steve would have to take me. Would he?

Eventually, he walked into the kitchen. I was steaming dim sims, his favourite lunch.

I said, not looking at him, 'Donte's in Adelaide and clown school is starting Sunday.' I turned round.

He was taking his cap off. He ran a hand through his hair.

'I'll need you to take me to Port Augusta because there's no bus from here tomorrow.'

He nodded.

'So you'll take me?' I asked.

'How else are you going to get there?'

I gave him a hug. He patted me on the back. So he still wasn't happy, but I was on my way.

Later that day, Steve said, 'Cid is asking if you want to come and stay with him and La Señora Mole in Adelaide Hills. He says I can bring down the ute for a service.'

'He's not asking, is he, Steve?'

'Sorry?' Steve scowled at me.

'He's telling us, ordering you to bring the ute for a service?'

'Oh, maybe. Anyway, you'll get to see Glencoe.'

Glencoe, yes, that was the name of the sheep station retreat in leafy Adelaide Hills. I'd forgotten about that place, their ivy-covered mansion in the Hills. I already knew Steve was going to say yes to Cid but I was curious all over again to see that vineyard farm at last, if not excited about staying there. However, the stay was going to be a compromise but – yes, I had to compromise. My solitary hotel retreat, gone; mixing with fellow students, gone; having a break from the husband, gone. All gone. I was relocating to another human hen house.

I agreed we'd stay at Glencoe. As long as I was going to my comedy school, it didn't matter, I had to reason. Plus, we were taking the ute, so it would take half a day to get there instead of the whole day by bus: a whole day by yourself, contemplating life, your life and… I had to stop that.

On our way to Adelaide, we passed a church whose sign said, 'An Olsh Church'. I asked Steve what kind of religion Olsh was. He didn't have a clue what I was talking about and then he said, 'Oh, it stands for Our Lady of the Sacred Heart.' OLSH Church! There goes the Aussie linguistic impatience again. No time to paint all those words on a sign, or even say 'Our Lady of the Sacred Heart'. Only in Australia.

We arrived late afternoon at Glencoe. Their driveway was a long, winding, tree-lined avenue through what looked like parkland. On one side they had brown alpacas in a meadow, and in the fields beyond were cattle, and in the distance, you could see the vineyard. The house had a circular lawn in front of it with weeping willow in the centre. This house wasn't falling down. Oh no – it was like something you see in Homes & Gardens, green, lush, expensive.

LSM was approaching the house from another stretch of road. She was with a young guy. She looked very country in her long wax coat, leather boots and Akubra hat.

Cid came out of the house with a stubby in hand and no shoes on. 'So, clown school for you, miss,' he said and grinned.

Steve said, 'Beers before five. You knocked off early.'

'Arrh, it's my first.' He held up his stubby.

LSM said, 'Be with you in a bit, eh,' and disappeared around the back of the house with her companion.

I was beginning to panic that I wouldn't make class for the six o'clock start. It had gone four o'clock.

'Come in, I'll show you around,' said Cid.

'Is it all right if I look around later?' I said. 'Sorry, I don't want to be late.'

Cid pointed to a garage and said, 'Take the Jeep – it's yours for the week.'

I could have kissed him. I drove away very happy, even more so because Steve wasn't coming with me. I was doing something on my own at last.

## My First Day at Clown School

As I was getting close to Adelaide, I was surprised to see it was surrounded by green fields and leafy hills. You could actually see the entire city. This was probably what London looked like, twenty miles out in medieval times.

The sat nav built in to the car directed me to the car park of the hotel where Donte's class was being held. My heart was beating fast when I got out of the car. Ten minutes later, I was walking towards the open door of the class – a stand outside with a picture of a cartoon guy holding a mic told me I was in the right place.

Donte was a black American, larger than life. He had on a trilby hat and wore a black suit and looked like a jazz musician. I knew he was going to be good, he oozed professionalism. We were five students in all, three guys and two gals (one student had dropped out). I took a seat and couldn't take my eyes off the mic stand at the front of the room.

One by one, we introduced ourselves and I liked every single person instantly for making me feel at ease by being friendly and open. Even the shy guy was ignoring his beetroot face and looking everyone in the eye as he told us what he hoped to learn from the course.

I was relieved when one of the guys volunteered to go first. He was funny too, and joked about having underlying medical issues that made him smell like week-old garbage.

I was second up, and my mouth was dry when I took the mic out of its resting place and moved the stand aside. I started with 'You might tell from my accent that I'm a Pommie…' I remembered it all, and so didn't stop till I got to the end, which felt like it took ten or fifteen minutes. My accents, from Scouse to Royals speaking in Essexese, came out strong. Sarah snapped her fingers and laughed her head off most of the way through my act. I loved that girl.

In reality, I only took four minutes because I was rushing through it so fast. My first lesson – if you have timed yourself correctly, don't rush your routine. Trust to the time and take your time, let people appreciate the joke. The slower the better. But you still need to aim for six laughs per minute.

I wasn't too happy about going alone to the dark car park, but I got in the Jeep without being attacked – yes, I was still timid in that regard. Oh well, I couldn't beat all my demons.

When I got back to Glencoe, Cid and LSM had gone back to their permanent residence, and the caretaker I hadn't yet met had gone to bed. When I asked what the guy was like, Steve started laughing but he wouldn't tell me at what.

He just said, 'You're in for a surprise.'

## Not Those Two Again!

Going downstairs for breakfast, Steve told me the surprise was that the caretaker had some of his family staying at the house. 'So it's a little crowded,' he said, still laughing.

When I went into the kitchen and saw two grey-haired oldies, I almost let out a squeal. It was the space-invading grey nomads who had set up their table and chairs opposite ours at the last caravan park we'd stayed at. I thought I'd stolen their grandson's job. But he had already got the job! I couldn't believe it, the caretaker at Glencoe was their grandson. Here was karma coming back to bite me again and teach me the error of my malicious ways.

We didn't get a chance to have much of a chat that day because LSM arrived with jobs for me and Steve – we were going to paint an outhouse. Yes, whether we liked it or not. I thought, what is it with country folk and keeping busy? But perhaps that is why LSM had four houses and Steve and I didn't have a pot to piss in.

I said to her, 'Did Steve tell you that we knew your caretaker's grandparents from our travelling days?'

She said, 'Yeah, he did.'

I said, 'They're lovely people.' Not sure why I said it. Maybe I wanted to appear kind.

But I laughed when LSM said, 'He's all right, but she's a little cunt of a thing.'

On day three of comedy school, we had a guest teacher, comedian Marc Ryan. He was going to listen to our full routines and give us advice on how we might improve. With his full head of hair and big beard, he looked like a grizzly bear, or Grizzly Adams. I got a shock when he took the mic and told us that he got into comedy to overcome his mental health issues. I looked at Donte, who nodded and smiled at me, yet I was about to poke fun at depressed miners for needing suicide prevention leaflets in their pubs!

I started to feel hot all over. How could I take the piss out of mental health when this guy suffered from mental health issues? But I had no choice but to carry on as before. Before I got up, I apologised for having possibly insensitive content in my routine.

'Hey, go for it – no taboos with me,' he said, which naturally helped.

When I finished, I could not believe my ears when Marc Ryan said, 'That was brilliant.' He sounded like he meant it too, and I have never forgotten how he said it and how it made me feel, and probably never will.

Donte had given me the strategies to succeed, should I wish to try out, and Marc gave me the self-belief I needed to chase away niggling doubts that I did not make sense to others. Steve, was he gaslighting me when he acted like I wasn't funny?

I did my stand-up. I got lots of laughs, then I was done. Had I spent that week alone, things might have gone differently. I might have made new friends, decided to try my hand at real stand-up. As it was, the only thing I wanted after that was to get back to Amirda. I wanted the space, the quiet, the time for contemplation. After a week of people and frayed nerves, I wanted to be alone.

## We Need to Have a Conversation

Back at Amirda, I was doing okay in my private world of thoughts, but Steve was not okay.

One morning after a silent breakfast, he said, 'Well, are you?' He was standing on the veranda in his boots and hat, water bottle in hand, ready to go somewhere.

'Am I what?' I asked, washing up the dishes way to slowly, trying not to show my frustration at not knowing what the hell he was referring to because he hadn't used a complete sentence again. It was a growing irritant, Steve communicating with me through telepathy. As a married couple of too many years, he honestly believed I could hear his thoughts and got mightily pissed off when I didn't understand him.

'Are. You. Coming. Out. With. Me. On. The. Water. Run?' he said with his teeth clenched in that ridiculously aggressive manner. He might as well have said, you coming to bug the shit out of me today, say you're too tired to drive or get out of the car? Are you going to whinge from trough to trough about how fucking hard done by you are...?

I didn't even know if I did it like he made out. Even so, I wanted to turn round and stab him in the throat with the knife I was washing in the sink. Yes, I admit not practical. That won't get the job done. Joking, just joking.

'Sure I'm coming with you, darling, don't you worry about that.' I took out the last of the cutlery and set it to drain – I hadn't even washed it.

He walked away muttering under his breath. I stopped myself from screaming after him, 'What's your fucking problem with every single thing I do – why is it you can be as miserable as death but I can't?' Was lockdown causing me to go mad. Nooooooo, of course not. Hahahaha.

I remember thinking, cricket season couldn't come soon enough, although it was months away. Steve and I were just getting on each other's nerves because we were seeing too much of one another, and something had to give.

And go on the water run I did.

It was all going pretty smoothly until we got up to the north end and Steve said, after checking on a tank, 'There's no water going in and it's half empty.'

I got out. It meant either that a pipe was blocked with shale or there was an underground break or leak that wasn't easy to spot. I puffed out air. We had heaven knows how many hours of lifting up pipes to check if there was water in one part but not another. I prayed it was a break. They're easy to spot.

When we couldn't find a break overland, Steve said while I was having a pee behind the tank, 'It might be underground.'

I was watching sheep having a pee too. I could have sung a song, 'and we all pee together'. I was also on the lookout for another vehicle. I was always dreading the time I was going to get caught out by someone. Here it might be Eastwood or Bella, as their place was close. Fellas are so lucky that they can pee standing up. They can aim right away from themselves. Squatting down near animal poop and flies wasn't the most dignified operation, that and trying not to soak your jeans.

I caught up with Steve, who was following the pipeline down to a creek. He had a shovel in his hand ready to dig up any ground that was wet. The sun was high and it was hot. I realised when my head started burning that I didn't have my cap on. I'm always taking it off in the ute because it itches when I sweat.

'Stay in the car for a bit,' said Steve. 'You don't have your hat on.'

I didn't need telling twice. I went back to the car, happy to get out of direct sunlight. I could have picked up my cap and run back to see him, but, I don't know, he didn't want me around. He was probably wishing he hadn't asked me on the run. When I think back, it was probably more me than him who was descending into a pit of woe-is-me of indulgent despair. But things were about to change.

With the windows down, you get a good breeze blowing through the ute. I was in luck today as it was eleven o'clock and Conversations on ABC radio was just starting. Richard Fidler announced he was talking to a woman called Cheryl Strayed. It didn't take long for my memory to be jogged when he mentioned that Cheryl's memoir had already been made into a film starring Reece Witherspoon, although I hadn't seen the movie.

As Cheryl's story unfolded, I couldn't quite believe what I was hearing. After the trauma of losing her mother, she decides she'll throw herself into a hike. Not just any little walk but she'll go right through the Pacific Crest Trail – that's like walking the Flinders Ranges. She starts in the Mojave desert with nothing but a backpack. All by herself, she hikes for days across a wilderness of forests and mountains. For fuck's sake, I couldn't even go to the paddock gate alone for fear of being eaten by lions, knowing that lions didn't even live there. She camps alone, washes in streams alone and does every damn thing alone.

Cheryl talked Richard through how she set off on her journey with a backpack so overstuffed that it was too heavy to carry and she toppled over.

Richard said, 'I can just see you laughing your arse off while you're on the floor.' Words to that effect.

I had to wipe a tear off my cheek. I don't know exactly what was making me cry. I think it was her freedom, her bravery – and now she'd gone through it and had this wonderful presenter sharing her story with the world. It was hard not to think of myself as a loser and my life a failed journey – yet I was in charge and I had failed. Yes, I had got on stage and done stand-up, but would I really ever go back and perform to a real audience? Did I even want to? And would I ever walk in the wilderness and not be frightened? When I was a child, I walked in woodlands alone and never gave it a thought. What had happened to me?

I was so absorbed with Cheryl's story and my own private reflections that when Steve got back in the ute and said, 'I found the leak,' I didn't know what he was talking about for a second. I also wanted him to shut up because I was trying to hear what Cheryl decided to ditch from her backpack so that she could carry it. Steve growled something under his breath and shut the ute door again.

Cheryl was then talking about how she was able to cope all alone on this extreme excursion into solitude because she had prepared herself psychologically. She had prepared herself – how? Damn it, I was ashamed of myself when contrasted to this bravest of women. Only the night before I'd lain awake for over an hour before I could summon the courage to get up and go to the toilet. And then it was only because Steve was awake. This woman could camp alone in a tent in a national park that she had never set foot in before. It was beyond my comprehension.

Cheryl's life story was shining a light on my cowardice. So many opportunities had passed me by because I was too afraid of the challenge. I was too afraid of motherhood and childbirth to have a baby. I left my lecturing job when they offered me my own course to run because such responsibility was making me sick. So many things were flying at me and then Cheryl was talking about taking heroin. I sat up. She took what? I realised something about myself again. I was transported to Brazil, where I met so many people who took drugs – cocaine mostly, but lots of other things. I was too afraid of unknown side-effects to take drugs. So again, I was basically a chicken. It wasn't through disapproval or anything. I was simply too scared. That's it.

This woman had taken, of all things, heroin. Didn't that stuff scramble your brain and make you want to eat your own flesh? Or was that crack cocaine? No, it was crystal meth. Whatever, it was all the same to me, those 'funny powders' had the potential to send you into a fit of crazed psychosis. But this woman had survived, oh, and now she thrived. She was in control of everything now. I caught my reflection in the rear-view mirror and saw my jaw had actually dropped open.

The news came on as Conversations took a break. I looked down to the creek to see if I could see Steve. He must be in the creek bed or beyond it, I thought, until I heard some swearing coming from another direction. It sounded like 'What the fuck?' Steve then appeared from behind the water tank. I got out and asked him what was wrong.

He said, 'Thought I'd found the leak. There was a water patch at the base of the tank, but it must have been sheep piss.'

I went to say, that was me, but caught my words. He was looking madder than a cut snake. Better let the woolly-backs take the blame. There was safety in numbers!

# I Know There Are No Lions in the Creek, Right?

Steve looked at me in surprise when he saw me decked out in running lycra and trainers.

'Yes, my arse is big in this,' I said before he could. I told him that I was going for a run up to the cairn that sits halfway to the first cattle grid.

Steve said, 'That's over two ks. You're going to run a five-k round-trip with that arse?'

This was our banter, or his banter. For years, we've been joking about how you can say the most outrageous and rude things under the guise of 'banter'. Example: 'God, you are one sorry excuse for a person.' 'Excuse me?' 'Just banter, love, don't get all arsy.' That kind of thing. We did have fun with banter, I have to admit. Something else I had to admit was that my belly was not attractive nor my arse either, which now had dimples in it. I could blame Steve for making me fat, or marriage, but he didn't have an arse like a sumo wrestler and I would not have been too polite if he did.

What I had not let him know was how much running to that cairn scared me. Actually, that's not true, I had mentioned my absurd timidity about going hither and thither alone, but it must have seemed so ludicrous to him that he dismissed it, and saw it only as an excuse for me not to exercise or go walking.

I wasn't entirely brave in my inaugural run that day because I knew that Steve wasn't going off the property. If I screamed, there would be someone there to hear me. I set off on a gentle jog, water in hand. My heart did start to pound when I was out of sight of the homestead, but I thought of Cheryl, who had talked about being scared and just accepting that you are scared. What of it? You just carry on.

Shortly after these elevated thoughts, I clipped a rock and fell on my face, badly scuffing my hand. Thank heaven for Cheryl, because I couldn't use the fall as an excuse to turn back. What was a little graze when that woman had crossed a state in makeshift shoes after losing her boot? I continued to the end point, reminding myself that animals run away from you, not towards you. Kangaroos do have a suicidal tendency to run directly in the path of car noise, but as I wasn't driving, so I had no worries.

I did some stretching when I got to the cairn and watched a crackle of cockatoos scatter when I yelled out to them. It felt glorious being alone with a creek to the side and mountains all around. I laughed until there was silence again. Then, okay, I got spooked then started legging it back to familiar ground, in case I was being stalked by an axe murderer. As I was fighting for breath and clutching my chest because it had a painful stitch, I knew I still had a long way to go before I was anywhere near having a healthy mind.

When I got back, my face felt like a bruised red plum.

Steve said, 'Well, you did run then.'

Yes, how about that, I had run all the way there and back. I'd made a start and I wasn't going to stop. It was nothing on the truly heroic scale of Cheryl Strayed. It wasn't deserving of a Chariots of Fire soundtrack, and for sure, Reece Witherspoon would not be chomping at the bit to make a film of my run to the cairn, but it was huge for me.

I'd like to say that I ran every morning before breakfast. That was never going to happen. No, I'd have my cup of tea, then breakfast, then coffee, and then I'd go for a run. I had a water pack on my back and soaked my hat with cold water when I got too hot. By the fourth week, I was starting to feel my body change.

I ran through August and all through to the cricket season. I felt great.

# Only Mad Dogs and Cricketers Go Out in the Midday Sun

Steve had been going to cricket training for only a couple of weeks before their first match, which was on home ground at Copley, close to Leigh Creek. Johno the policeman was there with a beer in hand because he'd clocked off for the day. Hopefully neither Leigh Creek nor Copley would have a crime wave that afternoon because the one cop was busy watching cricket.

The Aussies play cricket in summer. Hadn't anyone heard the song 'Only mad dogs and Englishmen go out in the midday sun'? It was the Aussies who were crazy, I thought. It was November and the temperature was already getting up into the high thirties. The match started at one p.m. and, with a cloudless sky, I wondered how they'd fare out there on the… I was about to say green, but Copley oval was not green, save for the run between the wickets. The rest was brown dust.

Indeed, much as I came to love it, Copley Cricket Oval (no less) is a patch of dirt. The spectators' area is a ripped canopy of tarpaulin, and the seating just racks of old school chairs. There is a bar. Its stocks of drinks are kept in a reclaimed shipping container around the back. Some of the wealthiest families along the Flinders make up the Copley Cricket team. One player, Tate, owns more land than the Prince of Wales, but is so modest you'd think he was one of his own workers. He flies his own plane, but at the same time shears his own sheep and musters his own cattle, and you can bet your life he fixes his own vehicles. He rocks up to play cricket with his boy and they share beers and jokes with anyone who cares to join in. Adam was another such man – big hat, handsome, ran a sheep station and would talk to everyone with the same big engaging smile. You don't see this in England, you just don't.

Copley Cricket Club is child-friendly too, although the wild Brumbies come and crap in the kiddies' sandpit. Regarding the clubhouse, it isn't exclusive, anyone can use the open facility for a picnic. Yet, for all its makeshift quaintness and quirks, Copley had won more trophies than any other cricket team for years, which is why Tyson, the president, is right to be proud.

As for the cricket team itself, the line-up was like something out of Dad's Army. Bush cricket is made up of players you might see if there was a war going on. It's as though the majority of fit young men have gone off to defend the borders and these were the men left behind – old, infirm, blind and crippled had to step in some days. Even kids and women (I know!) had to play when they were short of men. It's all part of the fun and uniqueness of this place – the outback. I exaggerate, but on some days, when farmers were not able to attend, that's a fair picture of the team.

At the interval, all the players were drinking beer, not tea. Too hot for tea, although the beer is what they call 'a mid', just 3.5% strength. I soon discovered that it's a little frowned upon to drink 'full strength' beer at 4.5%. Europeans will find this strange, because below 5% is not considered strong. The thing is, whereas I won't drink more than three or four beers, they will drink about a case each of the 3.5%. Warming up, during the game, after and beyond, they just keep drinking Gold or Northern. Given they were often playing in over forty-degree temperatures, I wondered whether guzzling so much 'lite' might be in case of a bushfire; they could put out the flames with their own piss. 'Drink Piss to Piss Out Bushfire' could be a slogan above the Copley bar.

I didn't get off to the best start when I met the cricket set. I mentioned the president, Tyson – when I saw 'Tyson' written on his sports shirt, I assumed that was his nickname at first. Now I know that Tyson is a popular Aussie name, but until then I had only ever heard of Mike Tyson.

I asked him, 'Why do they call you Tyson? is it because you're a fighter?'

He smiled and said, 'Nah.'

I said, 'Oh, it's the opposite. It's because you don't fight?'

Tyson said, 'It's my bloody name, eh.'

Steve broke away from a conversation he was having and said to me, 'It's a regular name here. Sorry, she's not being funny.'

The conversation moved on, but I felt some people suspected me of trying to be clever at someone else's expense. This got reinforced when I got chatting to some of the women. There were children running around them, playing a game.

The kids started friendly shouting at one little girl, saying, 'Don't put that ice cream on the seat, missy.'

But she went and put the ice cream on the seat.

'Aw, Missy, pick that up. It's dripping everywhere.'

I said, 'My mum used to call me Missy too when I was naughty.'

A couple of the women looked at me with frowns, which I should have picked up on, but I didn't and said, 'She's so cute. What is her name?'

'Her name's Missy,' was the collective reply, everyone looking a little baffled.

'Oh, right, sorry, yeah, of course,' I sputtered. Hand on heart, I thought that the 'Missy' in Missy Elliot, the singer, was a title, not a first name, like in Queen Latifah.

I swore that the next time I saw someone new, that no matter what they were called, even if it was Magic or Princess or Churchill, I would not take it for granted that it was their nickname or surname.

# I'm Getting a Stand-up Gig on TV!

I got a delightful shock when Adelaide comedian Marc Ryan sent me a DM via Messenger. He asked for my number because he wanted to discuss the possibility of coming up to Leigh Creek as part of an outback tour. He and several comedians, along with a TV crew, were planning a documentary showing the highs and lows of stand-up on the road. It was all hush-hush, but definitely happening. Could he ring me to discuss helping him set up a venue?

He most certainly could. I sent my number immediately and couldn't believe when he called me a few minutes later. I took the call out on the veranda where reception is best and prayed the phone call would work and not cut out.

'Yeah, thanks for this,' he began. 'Do you know of any suitable places where we could hold a stand-up show, the quirkier the better? I'd love to do something in a woolshed, say.'

'I'm looking at a woolshed,' I replied.

'Far out. That is good to hear.'

As he was talking, I was wondering whether or not I would be included. Would I get a slot or was this professionals only? Should I ask or was it too pushy? There was a TV crew after all, perhaps I…

'Will I be able to do my five minutes that you saw me do at the Laughter Lounge?'

'Oh sure, absolutely, yes…'

I listened to him with a growing feeling of possibility – why shouldn't I try stand-up – give it a real go?

Steve walked up, slightly shaking his head the way you do to show confusion as to what's going on. He must have known the call was something big. I wasn't going to interrupt my conversation to gush, 'It's Marc Ryan, the comedian from Adelaide.' Steve probably wasn't going to be too happy about me doing a gig in front of all the Copley and Leigh Creek folk anyway.

'We'll probably need to organise a liquor licence and some catering, and we'll need to sell tickets…'

I had to stop him there. This was bigger than me. I immediately thought of Jimmy from the Quandong Café in Copley. His father was on the local council and their family ran the community centre that Steve and I had never actually visited, to our shame. They did ticketed events and had a bar, I knew that much at least. I told Marc that I'd send him Jimmy's Facebook link.

When I got off the phone and told Steve what was planned, he was sceptical at first. 'Oh, it's just an idea they've got at this stage, is it?'

'No, it's going to happen as soon as I can get them a venue.'

An hour later, we were driving into Copley to see Jimmy, who was going to open up the community hall for us to see and take photos of. The Amirda woolshed was out of the question. It was too inaccessible to hold a public event – no one's tyres would make it, even if you could persuade people to travel all this way.

I could tell Marc wasn't too impressed with the town hall in Copley. It was a little too new, too done-up. It had just been refurbished and yes, it was like a classroom with its white tables that interconnected and its bright fluorescent lights that gave it all the ambience of a supermarket.

One of the things the documentary planned to capture was the messiness and shambolic craziness of outback gigs. Like in barns, where the locals jeer at the comics, 'My brother is funnier than you, ya fucker.' I got that a shiny new hall with rows of seated people like a school concert didn't fit the bill.

But there were other places, and I hoped that Jimmy would be able to put Marc in touch with the right people. Meanwhile, I worked anew on my routine and dreamed of getting my first break on the telly. I'd have to work on outback material – have a pop at the farmers. I could do something about outback Bunnings and how all a farmer needs is a box of shit and a welding cylinder to make a holding yard. Yeah, needed work.

# The Aussie Lingo

Fired up now about my comedy, and thinking this shit was getting real, I started working more on my outback comedy sketchbook. One focus was on language. My first encounter at the clinic when I went to get HRT patches had inspired me to develop some ideas further around the Aussie vernacular. I reread my notes.

> Vernacular: the language or dialect spoken by ordinary people. The shortening of words is a trait in the outback, even professionals go straight for the word-cut out here. A Flinders Ranges vet was on ABC SA radio talking about her experiences and encounters with more exotic animals. She was talking about her time with orangs in Borneo. Orangs – she meant orang-utans! Next thing, she's talking about how, again in Borneo, she enjoyed working with anthros. I was wondering what kind of animal an anthro could be. It was the interviewer who cleared this up when she said, 'You're talking about the anthropologists over there?' Never in my life have I heard a professional shorten academic references. But the Flinders vet did.

No doubt with this lady and her like-minded colleagues, 'conservation' is on its way to 'consa' if it isn't already there. I know the doctor – sorry, doc – is following a nationwide trend. We already have ambos for ambulance workers, firies for firefighters and pollies for politicians. The Salvation Army is officially the Salvos. Even a prime minister with a three-syllable name can't be linguistically tolerated, so Scott Morrison was Sco-Mo and Anthony Albanese, Albo. No wonder Aussies have no time for foreign languages. Spanish would explode heads with eight-syllable words like desafortunadamente (unfortunately).

Yet vet is short for veterinarian, so maybe shortening long titles is universal, depending on how much usage the word gets. Shoot, that won't help my comic angle. Nah, no need to reflect on that for now!

What I can develop is how Aussies don't like one-syllable words, especially in names. Steve or Dave are Davo and Stevo. If I say to Steve something along the lines of 'Did you believe in Jack Frost when you were a kid?' he'd say immediately, 'What, Jacko?' or 'Who, Frosty?' Aussie is a two-syllable language or tends that way. It's kind of cute, I'll give you that.

I love the Aboriginal lingo too. I was confused about 'deadly' at first. A public information commercial (pub info com?) had the slogan 'Keep your mob young, deadly and free'. Keep them deadly? However, like any word, the more you hear it, the less strange it becomes until it's the most natural thing in the world to hear 'It's too deadly, bro' and know it means something really positive.

Steve came back from the water run that day looking exhausted from heat and thirst because he hadn't taken enough water. To cheer him up, I began sharing my Aussie lingo thoughts that had occupied me that afternoon. For some reason, he didn't seem as taken as me by how egregious a sin to the English language was the cutting of anthropologist to anthro. Go figure!

## Can Rain Be Funny?

Marc Ryan was now in touch with the right Leigh Creek and Copley people, and he would keep me posted regarding a date for the gig, which was likely to be in about six weeks. Jimmy and I had been sworn to secrecy about the fact that a documentary was being made. We could say there was a camera crew, but it was to be played down so that the audience would think it was for the comics to see themselves. The last thing the TV people wanted was for the crowd to be on their best behaviour.

I was struggling with the comedy routine I'd perform. I couldn't do my accents, not the Scouser, nor the Royals sounding like Joey Essex, not that stuff. Steve assured me that the locals wouldn't get it, that Aussies don't have accents and wouldn't relate to the subject. I disagreed but didn't want to risk looking a fool.

The weather – what about that? Was it a potential theme for comedic development? Locals were obsessed with rain. People talked about it all the time. Steve had caught the habit and it made me laugh.

With Steve, his rain watching was very much of the glass half empty ilk. The day would start with him looking at his weather app. He'd say, 'Ah, it's all going to the south of us. We may get some but it won't do more than wet the ground.'

I would look at my own Google app and see that things looked more promising. When the rain did start to fall, and it was clearly heavier than Steve had predicted, he'd say, 'Yeah, but it will blow over too quick.' When the rain stayed, he would look out the window with a reluctant, 'Okay, better.' However, when he came to check the rain gauge, it would always be at least five mils less than what was needed. Even if it was over ten mils, he would get on his phone and say, 'Eastwood got twenty mils.'

I began to tease him about it. If I were accompanying him on a water run and there were rain clouds gathering, he'd say, straining his neck to look skyward, 'Wonder if Amirda will get any of that? Don't know if they're coming east. The BM or TC will probably get it all.'

Don't know how long it took me to notice this pattern of commentary, but one day, we set out and he began looking up at the darkening clouds in the distance.

After a deep intake of breath, I said, 'Don't think they'll be coming to Amirda, and if they do, what they drop won't be worth having.' I looked at Steve, who was frowning a little, seeming like he was getting the joke. I added, 'Just getting you started for the day, darling. Don't worry, I'll let you have the pleasure of repeating that ad infinitum all morning with varying degrees of pessimistic forecast for Amirda and optimistic hopes for Eastwood's place.'

He squeezed my knee hard at that spot where it makes you squeal because it tickles with horrible delight. It was one of those moments where it's fun, other times it drives you mad, this relentless negativity, the determination not to be pleased or satisfied or have reason to celebrate. It makes you want to take a running kick at the culprit's bum and launch them into the stratosphere.

Could I use that last idea about bum kicking in my act – would the locals laugh at that, and can conversations about rain be funny? I needed to find the answers before I took to the stage.

## I'm No Longer a Pommie But a PoMFA

It was December and we were in lockdown yet again – South Australia had another Covid cluster-fuck and the hospitals didn't have a spare oxygen tank to go around. Marc Ryan told me that the TV documentary was going to limit its reach to Quorn because that town was near Adelaide and if the venue was cancelled through lockdowns or limited to numbers, then they didn't have too far to travel back. Their plans for Leigh Creek and Copley were shelved. It was all off for me. I was not invited to participate in the Quorn gig, although, fair enough, I didn't ask if I could. In any case, it was too far for me and the same Covid uncertainties applied. I couldn't go all that way for it to be cancelled.

I went from being a playful dolphin splashing around in the great blue ocean of hope to a floating dead yabby in the creek of disappointment. I was even indulging, as you can see, in terrible analogies.

The tedium of station life hit me full force. I was lonely, bored and hateful, or hating my lack of a life. I seethed at being a PoMFA. Once I was a Pommie in lower case, an escapee from mother England. Now I was a PoMFA, a prisoner of mother-fucking Australia.

I told Steve to call Dan Murphy and place an order for a bottle of gin and whatever else I could think of to drown my sorrows. He refused to buy spirits at the inflated prices of the local tavern but agreed to the discount booze warehouse that is Dan Murphy's. Oh yes, Steve was only too willing to help me commiserate, and doubtless wanted to celebrate the fact that I wasn't going to make an unholy show of him in front of the Copley cricket team. I told him to order a swimming pool too. He thought I was joking. I showed him my phone. It was a picture of an inflatable pool from Big W. They delivered. So he got out the credit card and added a $20 inflatable pool.

A week later, we went to Leigh Creek to pick up a box of grog and a swimming pool. It was Saturday. I told Steve we were having the rest of the day off. That he didn't like, but I reminded him, or actually, shouted at him, 'It's not normal to never have a day off!'

Back at Amirda, Steve got a pump and blew up the oblong pool. Before filling it up with water, we tried putting it on the veranda, but it burnt my arse when I sat down on the thin plastic lining. We tried laying it on the grass, but the grass was too coarse and it was uncomfortable sitting on little spikes, plus the thing might get a puncture. In the end, we put down a canvas mat and got the pool up and running. Soon I was sitting under the hot sun, getting attacked by flies and overrun with ants. No matter, with a gin and tonic on a makeshift table – a trusty milk crate – I splashed the ants away and let the flies have a picnic on my face.

Steve got a text from El Cid asking him about the state of the yards. He was thinking about mustering in the new year.

'Is he trying to ruin our Christmas?' I said, trying to flick a fly out of my glass.

We had more drinks, and I was inspired to sing the 'Twelve Days of Christmas' song. Steve happily joined in and got out his phone so that we could remember all the verses. It wasn't long before we changed it to the Twelve Days of Mustering.

I went first. 'On the first day of mustering, El Cid did give to me… a pea-ea-cock up a gum tree.' (The peacock was still with us, by the way.)

Steve said, 'What about a dead ram in a gum tree? Remember from the floods?'

'Oh yes, better. On the first day of mustering, El Cid did give to me…a dead ram stuck in a gum tree. I like that.' I sang it a few times to get the rhythm right but eventually got the tempo when I put a hyphen between 'stuck' and 'in'. I said to Steve, 'Now you do the second day.'

He sat on the step and said, opening another beer, 'On the second day of mustering El Cid will give to me two cockatoos.' He was exaggerating the song's tune, which was making me laugh. 'Will that do?'

'That will do very nicely,' I said, tilting my glass at him. This thinking on the spot reminded me of our shop game from travelling through the Northern Territory. It was a weird porn shop, A–Z kind of mental challenge and I was enjoying it.

In the end our song went, 'On the twelfth day of Chris-a-mas El Cid did give to me…TWELVE drums exploding, ELEVEN pipes aleaking, TEN sheep aleaping, NINE emus racing, EIGHT cricketers drinking, SEVEN lambs ableating, SIX chooks not laying, FIVE dried-up springs! FOU-OUR thirsty birds, THREE cattle prods, TWO cockatoos, and a dead ram stuck in a gum tree.

We went in as the sun went down and I was lobster-red, which would make El Cid say, 'Serves you right you f-ing bludging piss-taking moles.'

## Oh God, Must I Do Another Muster?

TV in January: if you're watching I'm a Celebrity Get Me Out of Here… you probably have no life. The pastoralists and electricians-cum-I-do-everything, like Tyson and Hannah, had a life – they were on the set of Zac Efron's Gold out at Copley mine. Steve and I had seen the filming going on. We had gone grocery shopping in Leigh Creek and decided to go and see the much talked-about filming going on in Copley. We spied on the moviemakers, using Cid's rifle binocular that was always kept on the dashboard. Zac was in full acting mode, staggering around with a bloodstained face, cameras in front of him. Tyson stood by on the outskirts, smoking a ciggie. Bella was there with some of the other Copley cricket members.

I gave the binocular back to Steve and said, 'I need some drama in my life.'

To that, Steve laughed and said, 'It's overrated, baby,' and drove off.

I looked at him and thought, as if you have some greater knowledge than the rest of us as to what constitutes a full life. I looked back at the film set as we were driving away. I wanted to imagine that my novel Locked in One Nest might be made into a film, but I was getting a really bad feeling now about Sofia's representation. If I was being honest with myself, I'd had the sinking feeling since the beginning when I signed the agency agreement letter. A book is supposed to go out to publishers in the best shape it can be in. Then why had I not been assigned an editor from the get-go? Why had she not called me to speak to me in person? There had been no fanfare of any kind like you hear authors talk about when they get their break with an agency. It is a momentous occasion in their literary lives when they get a call from an agent. I'd had no call. Nothing but a letter of agreement to represent me.

I stopped myself. I could not bear to think I had landed Sofia's representation for nothing. No, it was the times we were living in. I was overthinking things. Sofia was Sofia. It was a coup – Covid had delayed everything, but the glacial pace would pick up. Had to. I'd soon have news that she had a buyer. Maybe even a bidding war, the holy grail for first-time authors.

When we got back to Amirda, Steve had jobs in the main shed, and I was free to do as I pleased. I went to my favourite gum tree, stood between its parted legs and screamed, 'I'm still stuck on this fucking sheep station. Why won't something get me out of here?' I was definitely up a gum tree in a bad way now. I was the frightened possum, panting for breath and scared for its life in case the hounds managed to jump up and swipe it out of safety. The dog going after me was 'mustering time again'. I was letting off steam before the muster. I just knew it was going to be stressful. It was hot as hell, windy as a typhoon and I could already sense frayed tempers because the forecast predicted no change.

Cid gave us plenty of warning as to when the second muster would be. Steve prepared the yards well in advance and I was prepared to muck in again by following everyone around in the truck, trying not to overturn the ute while crossing a perilous creek or rocky gorge. Cid was bringing some workers up with him to help in the yards. Was it okay if they stayed in the house because there would be people staying at the shearers' quarters? Not great, but as it would only be for a few days, we agreed – not that you really have a say in these matters.

I was surprised when Cid told us that his wife wasn't coming up.

He said, 'Do you mind being the lady of the house again?'

I felt I could read in his eyes 'and promise not to have a screaming meltdown and run away in my car?' I told him there would be no dramas this time. He was sensible enough not to bring a case of wine!

However, there was soon drama of a different kind, a serious one. The musterers came across dead goats with their guts all over the place. They had been shot, seemingly for the hell of it. There were also patches of blood showing that goats had been shot and taken. It was a slaughter-fest out there. Cid suspected the licensed roo shooters and was going to leave it. But Steve came across a busted trough that a car had run into. He caught up with the vehicle by following the tracks. It was the guys from Urdlu and they had dead goats in their truck, but Steve thought he saw a sheep in the back of the car. El Cid said that taking goats was their right, but not a sheep, he wouldn't stand for that.

That evening, Cid went to see Sherrie, head of the family at Urdlu. She spoke to her boys and swore that no way had they taken a sheep and said that they had not hit any trough either. Cid came away seething. Interestingly, he never called Aunty Sherrie any awful names, certainly not the C word. It was as if he still had his boyhood respect for the now Aboriginal elder. He swore plenty about her boys, though, and drank more Jack than usual that night.

I tried to lighten the mood by regaling everyone with tales of Broome sunsets and how they are like a laser beam in the eye. 'They're not like the gentle Flinders sunsets.' I starting asking if anyone had seen a sunset in Western Australia, like, say, at Broome.

One had, the pilot of the helicopter (no gyro this time, it was the zip-zappy 'don't mind cables overhead' copter-man). He nodded, laughing, and said, 'Yeah, they blind all right.'

I said, 'Jesus, it nearly blinded me looking at the fireball up so close. The first time I looked at it without sunglasses, I couldn't see properly for a full ten minutes after. Seriously, I was stumbling around like a fucking blind man.'

People didn't look too interested but I was determined to get a laugh and said, 'This kid hadn't fared any better than me and was going around with his hands outstretched in front of him crying, "I can't see."'

This got a little chortle from the tired musterers, so I carried on talking about how extreme Australia can be. 'I think it was that same kid who, the next day, was looking at a sign at the entrance to the beach that said "Beware Crocodiles, Beware Sharks, Beware Jellyfish, and Beware Rip Tides." And if you can brace yourself to get into the shark fin soup, do be prepared, if you're not an Olympic swimmer, to be swept out to the Tasman Sea.'

When I got the faintest of smiles from around the table, I tried to reassure myself that musterers and country folk in general were not my target audience.

And here, I would like to say RIP to the lovely helicopter guy I called Señor Helicoptero, which he liked. He was tragically killed a few months later when his helicopter literally dropped out the sky due to the gears seizing up.

## The Hokey Cokey Yard Dance

By day five, there was just me, Steve and Cid to do all the yard work. I hate yard work, just hate it, and I can now speak from experience because I was forced into the thick of the action and got no respite from dawn till dusk. For those who aren't familiar with it and may even have an idea that it's the stuff of rodeo legend and romantic cowboy capers, let me put you right by telling you what yard work is like.

For my experience of it, I was always in the wrong place. When the sheep are being moved from one pen to another, or Cid's trying to move them into the race or along the race, I am forever getting in the sheep's way. Cid yells at me to get back, but the problem is I don't know where 'back' is half the time. I end up doing the 'Do you mean here or there?' shuffle dance. It's a bit like the hokey-cokey: you put your right leg in? No! The sheep can see you. Oh, so it's your left leg out? No, that's worse. Okay, so I'll just do the hokey-cokey and shake it all about.

Except, absolutely no one is going to laugh your mistakes away with a silly song when you try and make light of not knowing what the fuck's going on. No, not when rams are trying to leap out of the yard because you've spooked them and lambs are cowering because you've scared them. Then he's yelling, 'Don't shout!' or 'Chase them in', or 'Don't chase them in there.' My nerves are shattered about five minutes in. At times, I suspected Cid was making sport of me, and a blood sport at that.

The one golden rule about drafting, as far as I can tell, is never leave a gate open. Because an open gate, and yes, folks, this was me, means drafted sheep will mingle with the undrafted and you have to start all over again. Don't tempers get nice when this happens. It's a soul-destroying moment, and I didn't dare look at El Cid until the redraft was finished and a modicum of good temper had restored his humanity.

Then there is the art of using poly piping to guide the sheep hither and thither. Should be easy enough, right? Wrong. When the sheep get backed up because one at the front has turned around instead of going into the race, that's when Cid starts yelling, 'You need to turn them around.' Fark, with a lot of confused sheep and clouds of dust making it hard to see and breathe, both for you and the sheep, bedlam ensues (which is why this was Bedlam paddock). Talk about the grit in your eye. Steve had to get in there and physically move them, then I get yelled at to move back so the sheep can't see me. Having to stay out of sight is a constant dance you do when you are also having to get them to go somewhere.

When the sheep start moving, Cid shunts a dividing gate this way and that way so that the sheep are divided into big and small, short and tall, rams and ewes, pinky and perky, whatever. It will be the first of many such drafts as they are subdivided. More dust, more yelling, more angst. Finally, you get to the point when the sheep are ready to be tagged, nutted, bobbed, perhaps all three. Then the fun starts in earnest: the choking dust, the leaping rams, your water in the wrong place so you can't get a drink when you're dryer than a nun's nasty. Then some essential piece of equipment has been forgotten and left behind. Lots of mole-cunt gets aimed at you as you race back to the car to get whatever is super-urgently needed.

I began to fantasise about turning the cattle prod on Cid, shouting with bloodshot mad eyes, 'See how you like being zapped in the neck, ya crazed psycho.'

It felt like I was constantly having to run back to the ute to fetch essential equipment like a plank of wood with clamps either end. It looked like something used by the first settlers that should have been thrown out long ago. It was the shelf for resting sheep on while they got nutted. The hold-all tin that accompanied the shelf contained a tub full of the smallest rubber bands I'd ever seen. They were for the purpose of castrating. I wondered how the hell Cid would get his Cumberland sausage fingers in those minuscule bands to open them up. I didn't realise there was a prongy tool for the job where you put the rubber band over four pins then, hey presto, Cid squeezes a lever and the band opens right up. That was another of my jobs, to fit the rubber band ready for nutting. Again, Cid was not at his best and would huff and puff like I wasn't quick enough or, if the band didn't go around the nuts and pinged off, it was somehow my fault.

Tagging is super stressful. Cid barks what colour Amirda tag to pull out and you must load the gun in quick time. Some sheep have lost their tag and need an old colour, which I have to go searching for while impatient Cid blows smoke out of his nose at my slowness. Same deal if you're not quick enough with handing out the general tags to him, he starts with 'Sometime today would be fucking nice.' I have to say, he always apologised for his bad temper once the task was done.

Naturally, to avoid the verbal assaults, I got the hang of loading the tag gun quickly, and dipped them often in the disinfectant before Cid lashed the gun in the bucket himself, growling about me giving the sheep rot with septic tools. I must admit, it's not an easy job having to clamp a sheep's ear when it's thrashing its head about trying to get away.

Yard work is hell, is what I'm trying to get across, like when Cid had to get in the race himself so that he could straddle an unruly sheep to clip its ear with its new tag. That is where it can get really nasty, like when a big ram from further down the queue makes a leap for freedom but only manages to fly into El Cid, nearly taking his head off. Dorpers are not docile like merinos, they won't go without a fight.

Cid yells, 'Steve, keep that fucking ram off me before his horns rip me a new arsehole!'

That day, I had to turn away and hope my convulsing shoulders didn't give me away. The mood Cid was in we'd have got our marching orders – well, until he'd calmed down and returned to his docile self, which was usually as soon as he'd stepped out of the yard.

The whole tagging process is bedlam – that word again. The poor sheep are getting crushed and coughing their lungs out with ears bleeding from the rough piercing. Then there are those who are struggling because they've got a small rubber band around the base of their nuts or daggy tail. At least the dorper sheep didn't have to be crutched like the merino. That's not nice to see. Their bums are shaved till they bleed so the wool doesn't grow back around their bottom. It saves them in the long run, more humane than leaving woolly sheep with a daggy bottom that will become flyblown and infested with maggots.

That same day, just when I thought it was all over and we'd be heading back for a cold beer, Cid asked Steve to help him get the weighing machine from the woolshed. He said, 'Sorry, my bad, I forgot.'

He forgot? I could see dark confusion on Steve's face – his thoughts were mirroring mine. Forgot what exactly? If that machine was coming out now, it meant all the sheep would have to be redrafted in order to line them up in the race, to be put yet again through a frantic queue, this time to be weighed. The weighing contraption had been in the woolshed for a while and we thought it was busted. Our worst fears were confirmed when we were headed back to the woolshed to load up the bulky weighing machine that probably didn't even work – hey, I was praying it didn't work.

Turned out Cid had got the thing going. Even the computer for recording each weight was operational – of course, El Cid could fix anything. Except this time, I was refusing to be impressed. So there we were again, poly pipes in hand – into the first holding pen to move the sheep from pen to pen. Cid once more making his whoop whoop noises to get a herd through the gate, all the while screaming at me to close the fucking thing before the sheep bolted back. That gate closed, another one to be opened, keep the sheep flowing into the race, close the gate on them.

'Aren't they too squashed in?' was a question I shouldn't have asked. Cid just swore oaths at me that I thankfully couldn't hear. However, one plus was that the sheep drafted much easier now. There was a flow to getting them in the race because they were used to it.

Cid was in charge of the weight recorder device and Steve in charge of lifting up the gate partition to let the sheep enter. But then things turned hairy again when the weight recorder malfunctioned. As Cid swore at the thing, the sheep grew restless in the race. Then Cid, for God knows what reason, took a call. It was hot and the sheep were crammed in that line, getting more and more restless and jumpy. One ram at the back had fallen onto his hind legs and his neck was squashed to the side. I wanted to signal it to Cid but I'd done so before and he'd ignored me and, in any case, he could see it all for himself.

When at last Cid got off his phone and was ready to go again, I saw that the ram with the strained neck didn't get up when the sheep in front moved up. Shit, he was dead – he'd been trampled to death. His eyes were staring at me, its mouth open. I called Steve to come have a look at it. He looked at Cid and Cid threw his hands in the air.

That rattled me and I shouted, 'The ram is dead!' I wanted to say, 'And it's your fucking fault, Cid, for pissing around on your phone.'

Sure enough, Steve confirmed the animal was dead. Cid came over to investigate. He yelled at Steve to get the thing out. Steve, with some difficulty, managed to drag the dead ram out of the race. It was an impressive creature, big and white with fine horns.

Cid booted it hard in the guts and said, 'That's for costing me two thousand dollars, ya useless fucking mole.'

Steve, like me, looked horrified. Cid was all but frothing at the mouth.

Cid stomped off back to the weighing machine, saying, 'Come on, don't just stand there, back to work.'

We continued until sundown. I don't know what outback station Mandy Magro based her romantic Rosalee novels on, but it wasn't Amirda, that's for sure.

## Am I the Barmy Army or Just Plain Barmy?

The away cricket match at Quorn was interesting because of the farm vehicles the cricketers travelled to the match in. Quorn, being closest to Adelaide of all the cricketing venues, meant that most pastoralists from the north were killing some kind of bird with a stone, mixing business with pleasure. There were trailers full of sheep to sell, or trucks full of hay that had been picked up from Adelaide. There were utes with bikes or tractor parts that needed taking to a city mechanic for parts and repair. It made sense to make use of it when you had travelled hundreds of miles.

As they set up for the match, I took a seat. Bella and her journalist sister were going to score. It would be impressive to see how they managed scoring with kids climbing all over their knees. Some of the other women were organising equipment or just catching up with each other's news or talking about another social event that needed organising. I wished I could make some contribution, but my life didn't cross paths with theirs. I remember thinking that maybe I should turn up in a Nelson costume and start singing in a thick Yorkshire accent, 'Who are we? Where do we come from? We are the Copley. We are almighty, the almighty barmy Copley.' Perhaps I would even get a little trumpet and blow raspberries in between nonsense choruses. I had those thoughts at Quorn because I stayed most of the long drawn out cricket day at the grounds. Much as I loved to see cricket life, it was good to go and explore the sights an unknown town offered.

No offence to Quorn (and yes, I'm going to be very rude about it all the same), but I find it's a dull place. I liked cricket matches at Blinman because it's pretty up there in the mountains. There are scenic walks to springs and places of interest all over. There's a mine you can take a tour of, and historical artefacts like the horse-drawn grader to have a look at. There's a funny story attached to it too: the man at the back would throw stones at the head of the man up front to tell him if he was veering off the straight line. I imagined how someone could abuse that channel of communication.

Talking of communication, I learned at that match that there was a concert coming to Leigh Creek. Copley Cricket Club were running the bar. I felt included when Tyson, the president of the club, asked if I was interested in helping run the bar. I jumped at the chance. After that, I was happy to stay and see the cricket game through to the end, although I was met with suspicion when I asked who won. Well, I wasn't keeping score. It's not like football where there's a clear 2–0 or 1–2. With cricket, when you ask what the score is, the reply is some 'four for this and two for that and he's yet to make an over' or some baffling breakdown that's impossible to follow. But I digress. A concert was coming to Leigh Creek and I was going to help run the bar. I was getting involved in the local life at last.

I was super excited that a concert was coming to Leigh Creek. That it was country and western music didn't appeal so much, but there would be people and music and something happening.

Our resident cop had told Tyson that the city police would be in force and they'd set up a road block and breathalyser. Therefore, it was strictly no drinking and driving this night. I laughed at the way Tyson put it when he said, 'Johno said they're setting up a breatho, so take it easy, eh.'

Many of the locals were there in a different capacity, showing another string to their bow. Helen, who ran reception at the clinic and manned the pumps at the gas station and worked the bar at Leigh Creek Tavern, was doing the catering that night. Hannah was selling her jewellery as well as running the bar and doing the books and the thousand other things. Eastwood and Bella were running a home-made food stall and her sister was chronicling the concert for the local paper. Someone was taking care of the kids in a trailer and looked like the child catcher in Chitty Chitty Bang Bang (why do I keep referencing that movie?). Eastwood gave me a warm smile as he did whenever I came across him. I often wondered if he ever told anyone about the day he saw me in El Cid's car trying to make my escape from Amirda. No one would have been shocked, because I daresay it wasn't uncommon around these remote stations.

Owing to another snap border closure in South Australia, none of the original line-up was playing. Tonight's bands were all local, and thankfully the ticket holders showed up all the same. The place was soon rocking and I was trying to keep up with the orders for wines, beers and spirits and not give people a can of West End beer when they wanted a Gold.

We weren't planning on staying. I was designated driver, but as the night got busier and louder and we had the offer of a bed at Tyson's, who lived in Leigh Creek, what the hell, once off bar duty, I had a drink, and then another and then… Well, everyone was handing out drinks left right and centre. You couldn't turn around without finding a drink in your hand. The Copley mob work hard and play hard and if you can't keep up, keep away. It didn't take long before I was asking Johno the cop why he wasn't having a beer like normal. It was a joke, but the Adelaide mob didn't find it funny, nor did they crack a smile when I asked if they were the Adelaide filth or the Port Augusta filth. My last memory was yelling at locals (to be heard over the music) that I didn't used to like them and found them aloof and creepy, but now they were all good. Steve had to move me on quite a bit.

We passed a mum yelling at her daughter, who was called Magenta. Magenta was another name I'd never heard of. Ruby, yes. Jade, of course, but Magenta – never.

The mother was yelling 'MaaaGenTaaaa!' trying to get her daughter's attention over the music.

I said to the mum, 'Ma-gen-ta is three very aggressive syllables in the wrong mouth.' I was keeping Steve very busy.

Back at Tyson's, everyone started shot games. I was doing more yelling at people about how I was a stand-up comedian, which no one believed (I don't think they communicate with Jimmy much), or perhaps it was because I wasn't the least bit funny when I said, 'Yeah, everyone fancies Eastwood, but you'd go right off him if he started doing that Midnight Oil stomp.' I mimicked Peter Garrett doing his straight-jacket dancing with his arms ramrod straight. I got some laughs, but I think it was at me.

The next morning we snuck away before anyone else was awake. You know when you've made a fool of yourself and don't care to see it in people's faces? Or maybe that's just what happens to me when I drink too much. I blame the fact that I was overstimulated by all the novelty and excitement of the concert. Well, that's my story, and I'm sticking to it, as they say.

The next time I saw everyone was at Copley gymkhana. I was whacked with the envy stick once again when I saw the cricket club in yet another guise. Now they were on horseback, the kids too. Wow, they could ride, and some. Our neighbours from Urdlu were there, as was Auntie Sherrie, who gave me a wave – we were on nodding terms at the post office and shops, although hadn't had any real conversation beyond pleasantries about station life and the weather. Her sons and daughters were amazing riders. Then they were all on bikes, again the kids too, doing daredevil stunts on planks of wood precariously balanced on oil drums, plus so much more. Even little Missy was on bikes and horses. Wow.

I bought a farmer's shirt with the Copley logo on. It has the Pilbara mark of the small Southern Cross windmill embroidered on the flap of one pocket, which, incidentally, has a gap in the seam so that you can stick a pen in there when it's buttoned down. I love my baby-blue Copley shirt, and the memories it stirs. It's now a souvenir.

## Sheep Shearers Are Sooooo Cool

I was looking forward to going over to TC again. We were going to collect dorpers that Eastwood had mustered along with his merinos. He had a team of Kiwi sheep shearers doing the shearing. He could shear himself, but you need a full team to get the job done right, and he was busy with other work like crutching and yard tagging. I was finally going to see an operational woolshed.

On our way up to TC, we would fit in a water run. It was going to be a very long day, but I was up for it. We were away by seven o'clock, trailer successfully attached to the ute. There was a flat tyre to be changed, a tow ball to find, and what felt like a million bolts to be tightened, but eventually we were on our way, lunch box packed, waters in the ute.

When we got to Camel-foe, we saw the Urdlu horses. They were drinking from the trough, all six of them. They were getting thin. You could see their ribs now. To make matters worse, the water tank was almost empty. The wind hadn't been blowing for days.

'Don't tell Cid?' I said to Steve.

'No, I won't, but he'll see for himself when he comes up and takes his usual tour of the troughs.'

'You hear that?' I said looking around.

Steve said, 'That's a car.'

Sure enough, in the distance, a vehicle came into view, then another. Two of them driving along the public access road. Sitting in the back of one ute were guys in camouflage khakis with matching hats. They looked like SAS commandos.

'They're probably going to Kurra Weena, a hunting group maybe. There's a load of goats about,' said Steve.

When we got to TC, music was blasting out of the woolshed. Bella was in the yards drafting the shorn sheep. She told us Eastwood was in the woolshed and that's where we headed.

It was a kick to see everyone working together and the merinos waiting patiently to have their haircut. Two women in short shorts and vests were classing the wool, one older guy was bagging it up with the help of a compressing machine. Four guys with mullets were shearing, using an electric razor suspended from above. They make four dollars a sheep, and shear about two hundred a day. They had been working steadily for five days already. This was a team who went about the country together, from state to state, and a pretty cool bunch of folk they were. I took a few videos on my phone. Yeah, they were really cool.

Perhaps merino sheep liked the music because they weren't making much noise, not calling out for the lambs they were missing outside. Funny, the huge merino sheep look a fraction of their former selves as they exit the shed bald, with small shaving cuts.

Then the rains came and there was much talk about how wet the sheep were getting outside. I wondered why all the concern – was it because of muddy hooves? No, their concern about wet sheep came from the fact that wet wool or wet sheep mean that the shearers get sick when shearing. I assume this has something to do with friction and lanolin oil. In any case, it is harder to shear the fleece and more dangerous for the sheep. Upshot was, they would be finished earlier and get a nice long rest.

On our way home, we heard shots in the distance.

'That'll be those Rambo guys' said Steve.

I thought again about those truckloads of guys with rifles. The problem was, they would be shooting more than just goats.

## It's Aussie Cricketers Who Are Barmy

The cricket final was to be a home match and Copley had made it yet again to the final. Whether Copley won or not, there was going to be a party for the end of the season at Copley pub. There was accommodation at the pub, but not enough for everyone, so many were bringing a swag to sleep in the back of their ute.

Copley won and so became champions of the Northern Flinders Cricket League. The shields were awarded and everyone proceeded to get shit-faced. It was probably just as well that the opposing team didn't stay around until the end, because they would have witnessed what can only be described as vandalism on the trophy shields. Tyson, as president, was custodian of the shields and paraded around the pub bashing the shields together like they were symbols and he was leading a marching band. When he stopped near you, everyone gathered around. This was the moment when the shields would be placed together over someone's face. The group would pour their drinks into your mouth via the funnel created by the two shields.

When it came to my turn, I closed my mouth and got soaked. A closed mouth was breaking the rules. A new group with new drinks was called. The shield was placed over my head again and when I didn't open my mouth, my belly was tickled. This time I copped the lot, and drank copious amounts of God only knows what.

When the shield ceremonies were done, people's clothes started to come off and the next thing, several of the cricket team were naked on the bar doing weird prancing around while everyone screamed, hooted and cheered. I began seeing double as I was trying to focus on who had the biggest dick, but really couldn't tell.

The last thing I remember was staggering round trying to find our ute. I couldn't find our swag. I passed out on the back seat.

I woke up to see Steve standing at the open door, saying, 'I thought you must have gone off with someone.'

I had completely forgotten that we'd booked a room!

I got out of the car to the sound of snoring. I saw it was coming from swags in the back of utes.

I said, 'It's like a ute motel in the car park.'

Then I noticed a few puddles of vomit. Despite the vomit, it was something to see this open-air dormitory. Thinking of this scene and the sheep shearers experience, I felt that the country set here were a cool set of people indeed. It was about time I did more tweeting and let the rest of the world know.

# The Horses – and Horrible Symbolism

The first thing I did on opening my eyes was the same thing I'd done the last two mornings. I reached for my phone. I stared at the screen, looking for the telltale heart announcing that someone or some people had liked my sheep shearers tweet, along with a bunch of others. I had retweeted it with a few more hashtags like #outbackexperience, #loveAustralia. I stared at the screen, not believing there could be zero response. But there wasn't even one. Wait, perhaps I needed to kick-start the Internet. I tapped the blue bird. Oh, Twitter was reloading. I looked at the top of the screen for the hearts to start popping up. Nothing. I put my phone down and picked it up again. Nothing. Should I delete it? It was worse than people not liking my post about sheep. It said that not even my friends were following me. Damn. No one gave a shit.

The next thing I did was to pen an email to Sofia, asking her if anything was happening with my novel. 'Just touching base to see how your pitch of Locked in One Nest is going.' I felt that it might be pushy, but for heaven's sake, shouldn't she keep in touch just a little bit? I sent it before I could talk myself out of it.

Steve rolled over and patted my back and said, 'Water run today. Who's making the sangas?'

I groaned inside. 'I'll give you that honour,' I said, trying not to sound down.

He didn't seem to have time for the doldrums lately. Oh grief, another water run, another month of a life going nowhere. The window rattled and something banged outside.

'The gale-force winds are back,' I said, getting up.

'Been blowing a gale most of the night. Should mean Camel-foe tank is full again,' said Steve, stretching.

An hour or so later, I was getting out of the ute to open my first gate, the one that took us to Camel-foe. 'You'll need to cut back those bushes,' I said as I was closing the ute door and nearly getting blown away.

Talk about from one extreme to the other. From not a breath of wind to a tornado. Dust swirling up in a big whirly-wind made it difficult for me to see the gate lock and when I pushed it open, the wind took the gate out of my hands. Then I saw an emu that had been hidden by the overgrown bush. It pulled back its head but didn't move away. I stepped out of the way so that Steve could drive through the gate. It was then I noticed the emu chicks, about five of them on the other side. Oh no, I had got between daddy emu and his babies. At that moment, the dad ran right at me flapping out his huge wings like he was doing an elaborate dance, but it was scary. I tried to run for the ute but the irate emu was now in my way. I stumbled back and landed on my arse. I tried to get up but the damn thing was still doing some agitated dance at me. I yelled for Steve. I saw him coming with a broom. I scrambled back up and had to walk backwards so I could keep my eye on the bird. The next thing I knew, I was falling, tumbling down into the creek.

'You got between Dad and his chicks,' yelled Steve, running down to the creek.

Then there was more confusion. Both of us were gagging because of some stench.

'What the f–' I started to say, but couldn't finish. I was looking at dead horses. Those beautiful cinnamon horses were lying dead within metres of each other, all along the creek.

Steve ran back to the top, and I followed him, trying not to gag.

'The horses were dragged in there,' said Steve, looking around. He pointed to rows of tracks, then he ran back into the creek.

I didn't want to see the horses again and went to the ute. The emu and its chicks were now way along the fence line, still running.

When Steve came back, he said, his voice breathless, 'They've been shot. The big stallion had three bullets pumped into his skull. He mustn't have gone down –'

'Don't tell me any more,' I blubbed.

My phone kicked in, and there was a reply from Sofia. It would be morning there.

## It's Time to Go, But Where?

I have a memory that has no feelings attached to it. When I was eight, I got the bus from Liverpool back to my village in Halton, Cheshire. The distance was about thirty miles, nothing in Australia, but in England that involves going through a lot of areas. I had to change buses but then no bus came, so I ended up doing a lot of walking. I eventually got back to my village and went straight to the bungalow I used to live in and was missing so much. There was nobody home. I looked through the windows. I don't remember what I felt, but I was there for a long time. Then I went and sat on the low stone wall. I loved that wall, always warm if the sun was out. I sat looking at the field opposite that was used for weekend football matches. I had spent my whole life playing on that field through every season.

I was disturbed by a lady from one of the houses in the lane (this was Spark Lane, and our house had been called 'High Hopes' – the name had been taken down). The lady, whose name I forget now, asked me what I was doing. I remember the concern on her face as I told her I was visiting. She asked me if I had money to get back to Liverpool. I lied and said that I did have lots of money.

I don't know why I didn't have any money left or enough money, but I had to walk home and it began to get dark, then I got frightened – I do remember that. A man on a small motorbike, maybe it was a scooter, picked me up while I was about to cross the Runcorn bridge. He took me to his works office and the police came and picked me up. I remember begging the police not to tell my mum where I had been. I have no memory of what happened after that. I think the police watched me go in and that was the end of the story. I have no idea what happened that night, if my mother or father were even home.

The overriding sense is that from then on everything good in my life had gone. My mum had been replaced by someone I didn't recognise;

my dad was always sad; my brothers wrapped up in their own lives – or who knows, perhaps it was me who turned inward. I certainly caused my parents a lot of grief because I would fight, steal, lie, tell them and teachers that God was a joke, and act out almost anything that upset people. I do remember my mother constantly taking me aside for a stern conversation but the only thing I was thinking was, your breath smells bad. Was I just a brat? When my eldest brother, of course going through the same confusing hell, was expelled from school, it was the catalyst for change. Mum sold up and we moved back to the village. But Mum continued buying luxurious things we didn't need on credit cards she had no intention of paying off.

I love my mother, and we get along so well when I'm entertaining her at home. I've always been her entertainer as well as housekeeper/cleaner, and in those roles, she rewards me well both materially and affectionately. But she hurts me, despite the fact that she would do anything I asked of her. However, what I wanted was for her to take an interest in me, and that she seemed incapable of doing, which is why I couldn't share my latest disappointment.

It was these thoughts that dominated in the aftermath of Sofia's email. She had failed to sell my book. No one was buying it, nor interested in it. Nothing, nada, zero, zipalata.

'Your thriller is good, but not good enough to be a sure-fire blockbuster.' Her email was long and full of wholly negative feedback. 'Publishers are being difficult about acquiring new authors unless they believe it to be a bestseller… Maybe agents being furloughed under Covid has…'

She went on about me not having other books that she could put forward. She hadn't asked me for them! I have plenty of other novels that I've put to one side. Wait. She knows that. She's read them! Who was this joker, I thought. They were thoughts I shouted at the walls as I stomped around in shock and disbelief.

I packed up my laptop. I didn't want to be reminded of yet another futile literary journey. God, I was such a loser. Whatever path I took in life ended in a brick wall that kept me the wrong side of the life I thought I should have. I wrote an introduction to a John Kirby art catalogue, met lots of artists and writers. Did I get invited to one party? No. Did my intro get referenced in any of the magazines? No! All rather like the fate of The Unsung Artistry of George Orwell, ignored.

Steve would be so disappointed. He had supported all my writing ventures. God, what a chronicle of failure my writing history has been. After O Eve had been rejected by every single literary agency in England, I self-published O Eve under L T Saunders. It got five-star reviews on Goodreads, one pointing out that it wasn't a thriller but a contemporary romance with a crime subplot. I'll settle for that – but it has a killer twist. However, O Eve failed to sell because it got no marketing, as promised by the Yorkshire publisher/printer.

My other novel, Falling for Mr Knight (not as soppy as it sounds), suffered the same damp squib fate. Yet I paid good money, in the thousands, for printing, distribution and marketing, and that was nothing to do with design, editing and all the rest of it – I paid a handsome sum to others for that. They failed to sell one single copy, yet wanted to keep charging me annual fees in the hundreds to keep the boxes in storage. I should have stuck with Kindle.

Regarding getting a real publishing deal – that is, one in London – I concluded that if you set a story in Liverpool and it's not about a middle-class lawyer who lives on the Wirral, forget it, the London snobs won't go near your low-bred protagonist, unless she's a slum girl from the nineteenth century who married the son of a lord or some shit like that. In these unmeritocratic times, only a hero who is down and out in Edinburgh or Glasgow will interest London, who will love the rugged, even disgusting charm of your antihero. Just don't let them be English, that's a step too close to home. I hate the English class system with every undigested ounce of puke in me.

I see Steve and I taking all those boxes of books full of O Eve and Falling for Mr Knight, dropping them off at charity shops and bookshops to be given away. I put a sticker of my email inside every single book, and still to this day, not one person got in touch with me. I would conclude that I must be a bad writer if it were not for the Goodreads reviews and all the people unrelated to me who raved about both books when they had no reason to please me. Yes, both books had amateur flaws, which is why I unpublished them from the Kindle site, but I still feel a loss for those novels, like I didn't do them justice. They were my children and I let them down by not bringing out their full potential, essentially aborting them.

I sat down, my mind triggered again by – I don't know how to put this but suddenly I saw my mother in a new light – a young mother with three children she didn't ask for. It wasn't like she'd had IVF. A shotgun wedding at eighteen to a man she didn't love but whose arms comforted her while she was on the rebound from that police cadet she did love. She bonded with her firstborn, but her second one, me, she didn't bond with – I wasn't like her. I was like my father. We even looked alike. I was a female version of him. But she wasn't cruel, she simply wasn't that into me. Wow. That's it. No big mystery, no need to feel myself inadequate or especially hard done to.

But my child, firstborn, the Orwell book, I mustn't abandon it. I had to save her from a life of undeserved obscurity. Why, the eminent Professor Peter Davison, the late great Orwell scholar of all time, had supported me in the creation of that academic tome. He had fact-checked, suggested further reading, given me pointers of untold value. I had to do something. Routledge publishing house had bought out Ashgate and my contract was now with the new company. Routledge could bring out The Unsung Artistry of George Orwell in paperback at an affordable price, meaning it could be purchased in bulk by libraries and schools with stretched budgets. Finally, my book could reach the potential that had been promised to me. Routledge was sure to have a marketing department that didn't suck the big one.

I wrote to several literary editors at Routledge. My letter was impassioned. I talked about the prohibitive costs of the book set by Ashgate at over £100 and repitched what my book had to offer that was new and why it didn't deserve its pitiful fate. I finished the letter with '…I hope and pray you will be able to breathe life into a prematurely-dying academic voice.'

A few weeks went by and I began to get that Sofia feel. But I wasn't despairing. I was getting a taste for new life, new growth, new beginnings, new everything. Despite the routine of Amirda, I was now enjoying the physical challenges of weeding, log cutting, cleaning out troughs, and I kept on running. I had almost lost my fear of being alone in far-off places. I was never brave enough to go out to Mount Remote alone, I wasn't called to do so, but I had come a long way.

El Cid said he didn't know anything about the shooting of the horses but feared he would be held responsible. Steve told me about their conversation. Cid said that he wasn't bothered about the horses, but he was bothered about why it had happened on his property and about what Aunty Sherrie would say.

'How will she find out?' I asked.

Steve said, 'Cid reckons her boys will go looking for them and they already know where they've been hanging out, at the Camel-foe water source. It's just a matter of time.'

I was spooked by it. 'It's time to go, Steve,' I said and meant it. 'I don't like what's happening. If it wasn't the wild west before, it's going to get like that.'

However, Covid was far from done. There would be more lockdowns and state border closures. It was hard to believe, but another year went by, almost a repeat of what had just gone by – all our visitors came and went in much the same fashion. I was never alarmed when an unannounced car pulled up. It would be the meter reader, or the oil truck, or a lost camper, or someone popping in for a cuppa, or someone asking if they could go looking for fossils or camp for the night.

I was now well known in town and chit-chatted with the locals. We went to houses for tea and drinks in the evening on a few occasions.

Bella at TC always said, many times, 'You must come for tea.'

We never did. Such an unspecific invitation is done on purpose. El Cid and LSM got divorced – all super quick. I think she's in and out of rehab nowadays. It was she who divorced Cid when he said he wouldn't release funds for her to turn one of their houses into a beauty salon.

Despite how well we got on in our last year, I always felt an outsider because I was an outsider. We would leave and they would all continue. I saw that the families were not idyllic as they first appeared, they were human beings, and so husbands and wives alike could be frustrating, hurtful and mean, same as the rest of us. Still, they all looked to be stayers.

This was not my place to stay, so when Steve suggested buying the sports club that was closing down in Leigh Creek (and it was cheap), I said, 'You can buy it and live here, but I can't live here.'

He would not consider separating from me and so that was that. He asked me if it was because of my mother's health. That threw me. She had not been too well, chest infection after chest infection, but I assured him that my mother's health was not my concern, same as my ill health had never been anyone's concern but my own since I was small. Typical Steve, if I'm being distant, then he thinks it must be because of some problem outside of our marriage.

The water runs and daily routines continued as before – the cricket season came and Copley won again. However, Steve did retire and they gave us a good send-off, because we had both said we would not do a third year at Amirda.

At our leaving do, I was asked to say a few words. I now had a reputation for liking the public stage. I was glad to be asked, so when the rowdy drinkers at the match-win celebration said, 'Speech, speech' to me after Steve had received his short-service medal, I began with 'I was brought up to believe that if you have nothing good to say, you should say nothing.' This got a collective chuckle as people realised I was joking. Steve was not amused and had to be pushed back onto the platform to say his thanks.

El Cid was lovely when we handed in our notice and thanked us for staying so long.

Later that week, Steve said, 'What are we going to do when we leave here?'

'I'll go and see my mum,' I said. 'International borders will be open soon. We can have a holiday by the sea until then.'

'I've been offered a job,' he said.

'Oh?' I sat up a bit more.

'Yeah, it's a bit remote, but it's in a community, not lonely like here. It's in the Northern Territory. The nearest town is Katherine, 560 k away. Darwin is nearly 900 k away.' He stopped and looked at me. 'One other thing.'

'What?' My mind was whirring.

'It's a dry community.'

'Dry!' An involuntary smile pulled up my face. 'For some reason, I find that mighty appealing.'

Steve nodded and smiled.

'And you'd be doing what?' I asked.

'Works supervisor. It's a council job. Good money. It's in an Aboriginal settlement called Lajamanu.'

'How did you get a job in an Aboriginal community?'

'An old army mate is a ranger there. Look, I'll get us a couple of beers and tell you all about it. You can get a job at the school if you want – there's heaps of opportunities for teaching.'

I got out my phone to look up Lajamanu and saw that I had several emails and messages. The email that caught my attention was from Routledge, from one Michelle Salyga. Her first line read, 'It is a pleasure to be in touch with you…' She 'confirmed' that Routledge 'would indeed be bringing out The Unsung Artistry of George Orwell in paperback.' I was back in the game!

I got out of my emails and saw a message from my mum. The word 'cancer' stood out. 'It is lung cancer, darling. I am devastated. When can you come home?'

Steve came back in and handed me a beer. 'So what do you think?' he asked. 'Do we go?

www.ingramcontent.com/pod-product-compliance
Lightning Source LLC
Chambersburg PA
CBHW030227100526
44585CB00012BA/304